EARTH & FIRE

Modern potters, their tools, techniques and practices

Kylie Johnson and Tiffany Johnson

Contents

Foreword 6

Introduction 11

Earth and fire: A partnership 17

The language of clay 21

EARTH

 Throw 29

 Hand 81

 Cast 121

FIRE

 Flame 141

 Mark 181

 Form 229

Index of artists 270

Foreword

Vipoo Srivilasa

I always love to see how artists arrange their studios; whether they are messy or clean, filled with darkness or light, organised or chaotic. Studios are a window into an artist's practice and what inspires them. Not only being a place for creating art but also a reflection of them and what they choose to surround themselves with as they create. Look to the backgrounds to discover what artists are collecting themselves – I love a glimpse into another artist's studio life. You also might pick up some tips, discovering how another might hold a tool a different way, or arrange their process. The photos along with the approachable yet vivid detail of their practice makes this book enticing on many levels.

    Reading *Earth & Fire*, I discovered so many new artists that excite me. The range of cultural backgrounds, influences, skill levels and type of work is quite extraordinary. You can tell the artists in this book are highly skilled and enjoy what they do. My suggestion to you would be to read one artist at a time, let yourself reflect on their story, their process, and you will not be overwhelmed. Use the icons and technical information to cross reference other artists who use the same clay or fire to the same temperature, see how differences occur. We can all start with the same clay body but end up with very different work – that is the artistry of the individual.

    I'm sure you will, like I did, find the book to be approachable as a reference book and as a piece of inspiration for your own creative life. For me, reading it felt like visiting a friend's studio for a cup of tea with them. This book assures me that the future of ceramics is bright and secure, with many new talents taking on ceramics as their profession. There is a strong sense of community through the pages, as well as the message that sharing knowledge is a good thing because it inspires others. There should be more books like this, where we can feel reassured that having a life in art is valid and enduring.

Page 1: The work of Nicolette Johnson (p. 261).

Page 2: Asuka Mew throwing a vessel using a pottery wheel (p. 35).

Opposite: Sculptures from Vipoo Srivilasa's 2022 series *Always Better Together*.

Angus McDiarmid's studio and gallery (p. 143).

my epic love
always vivid
in every beautiful
mark of

my
sweetheart
stargazer

imperfect
and
absent

absent
and
everywhichway

when
the
layers
subside

and the fortune
is empty

the pigment
of our days will
echo pure

and i will be

n o w h e r e

if not with

you

and still
i
love
you

you orbit my life

at the bottom of my footfall... in every cloud that brushes by... deep within my pocket of these days i carry you with me...

In my
hand i had a
kingdom
in my hand i had
yours

maybe
geography
made
us
friends

Introduction

Kylie Johnson

Earth and fire: two elements that are the main components of any piece of ceramic. Mud and heat. Potters have been turning earth into stone for over thirty thousand years. Ceramics are one of the oldest human creations. In this book, we introduce you to some of the most exciting ceramic artists working today, and discuss how they work, what materials they use and their thoughts on the medium.

The book is divided into two sections: Earth and Fire. In Earth, we explore the process of building forms with the base material of clay, and in Fire we see how the alchemy of heat and finishes can create such diverse work. The sections indicate each artist's prime approach, and their specialties are identified with six different icons. **Throw:** wheel throwing creates forms by using the rotation of a wheel and guiding hands to construct a vessel. **Hand:** handbuilding can create a more organic result as the artists use their hands and fingers as tools. **Cast:** creating a cast is a technique used to form work that is not easily achieved on the wheel or by hand, and when multiples are required. **Flame:** bare flame and ash produced by a woodfired kiln can have a profound effect on the finished look of a piece. Glazes can also react in an electric or gas kiln which may affect colour, transparency and texture. **Mark:** while some ceramics have a quietness about them, others are defined by mark making. The clay is a replacement for a canvas and the artists use their unique marks, whether they be bold, metallic, symbolic, or satirical. **Form:** similar to mark, ceramic artists have a freedom to explore clay and how it responds when creating forms or sculpture. Fire can make or literally break these forms.

To create a book like this is no small task, particularly when deciding whose work to profile. To present the scope of work being done by contemporary ceramicists is almost impossible. Our aim is to celebrate ceramics and show how these artists create, why they work with clay, and where they pursue their craft.

My sister, Tiffany, and I selected artists from all backgrounds, ethnicities and locations around Australia. We included artists we have known for many years and whose practice we already know intimately, and others we have only admired from afar. We talked to career potters whose work has spanned decades and who are still working as passionately as they did when they started. Then there are potters and ceramic artists who have only been practising the craft for a short time, but have chosen it as a lifelong pursuit and are so dedicated that the quality of their work belies their experience.

We have chosen to share all types of makers, from exhibiting artists whose work is installation, non-functional and esoteric, to people who make plates and cups for us to eat and drink from. This takes in production potters to handbuilding sculptors, those obsessed about woodfiring to those who are highly illustrative and decorative makers. We hope this breadth of creatives shows the diversity of ceramics – at one point their work can be in a gallery and the next on a kitchen table. You can wear a pair of their earrings or arrange a bunch of flowers in their vase.

I have been a ceramic artist for thirty years and have been working solely in my own practice for the past twenty. For the past ten years (and counting), I have also had the privilege of owning and running paper boat press, a ceramic gallery in Brisbane that shows ceramics from around Australia and Japan. Being a maker myself and sharing the artform in my gallery gives me an understanding of both sides of the medium.

During my career, I have seen many changes. Recently I have witnessed an uptick in the popularity of ceramics. Over the past ten years, the gallery's customer base has become more informed – they now see more value in a handmade piece. This sentiment is growing around the world, which is why a book like this is so important for keeping that conversation going. There is a long way to go but I hope this book opens more hearts to the lengths makers go to, the time they put into their careers and the sheer hard work it takes to turn a block of clay into a form.

Previous: Poetry vessel greenware by Kylie Johnson.

The underlying thread we discovered as we interviewed these artists is that their intent is pure because clay demands that of them. They have a love and respect of the medium and recognise how clay is ancient, from the earth, it is turned into stone, and is also a mystery. It is for many not just seductive but meditative. Clay, in the end, is the greatest teacher. The earth and fire that the artists use to make their objects are the ultimate masters. Just when you think you know one thing, the clay, glaze and heat will teach you another. There will always be more to learn. Working in clay is, quite simply, humbling.

Sharing information and passing down ideas and glaze recipes is a part of the craft that I value more than ever after writing this book. The potters know they are not reinventing the wheel; they are simply trying to make something beautiful and meaningful, useful and valuable, that people can fill their lives with: drink from, eat off, look at, be inspired or moved by. And all of them strive to make good quality work that is considered, not wasteful. There is meaning and thought in their practice, and this is part of what they share with the world.

The joy of being able to make something that is loved by another, and which some of their spirit and energy goes into, is a sentiment we heard over and over. Many of the artists in this book are also teachers of the craft, and their stories and opinions have given us many insightful moments. They have a conscious consideration for the environment and are courteous to our Earth. They know that what they make will last thousands of years. Ceramics has a proud history and legacy spanning millennia, and part of the unwritten oath of a contemporary maker is to keep this history alive and pass on this legacy.

The ceramics industry seems to be in a renaissance, not seen for forty years. This is to be celebrated, especially in this fast-paced world. The quicker and noisier the world gets, the more we are turning to the handmade, the human connection. No other physical artistic medium connects you more closely to another person than a cup that you raise to your lips and drink from, that has the maker's mark, energy and love in it.

Clay is a teacher. An emotional rollercoaster. It is affected by the elements and weather in the throes of making. It is mud and it is cold. And then it is subjected to fire, and it is all about alchemy at that point.

Ceramics is a job, a career, a hobby, an art. It is for those who understand nuance but are also physically and mentally tough. You must be a magician and a renegade, and you must be patient. You must be flexible and open to mistakes and failures. You must always know that you are part of the earth, just like the clay is, and it will change you, just as a pot will change when fired.

I have always said that clay doesn't just get under your fingernails, it gets under your skin. This is evident in the life's work of the incredible artists featured in *Earth & Fire*. For me, as a maker, collector, gallery owner and writer, it has affected me in all these ways and countless more. It is our hope that after reading this book that you now hold in your hands, as you would your favourite handmade bowl or teacup, the beauty and wonder of clay will touch you all a little more too.

KYLIE JOHNSON

Founder | Creative Director
paper boat press

Following, left: Asuka Mew's wares drying on shelves (p. 35).

Following, right: Ray Cavill's kiln (p. 153).

Earth and fire: A partnership

Jane Sawyer

Clay is a wonderfully engaging material for humans. In our hands, it responds as if it were alive. Every clay feels different and behaves differently. They each have an individual personality, a character that demands the maker learn to work with it. This is a relationship, a partnership, that has allowed many aspects of human culture to be recorded throughout history. Today, archaeologists, ethnologists and historians around the world continue to learn from discoveries recorded in clay. From the oldest ochre cave paintings to the latest 3D-printed ceramics, our human journey is deeply connected to this unique material. And, like any good partnership, its future depends on respect.

Clay is made by and of the earth through thousands, even millions, of years of geological forces at work. Phenomena such as abrupt and violent volcanic eruptions, continental movement and earthquakes and glaciers in combination with acids, gases and water pressure are part of a complex weathering process that, over extended geological time, acts on rocks and breaks them down into fine particles of silica and alumina. These particles are often moved far away from their original source and become layered in deposits that result in clay as we know it: a pliable and responsive material that can be dug straight from the earth.

Humans are the lucky recipients of this remarkable natural material. In its plastic state, clay is responsive to all the delicate nuances our sense of touch can offer and it can be used as a paint, a powder or a solid. When fired in a kiln, it becomes ceramic. It turns the clay from mud into a durable material that can last thousands of years.

The invention of the kiln transformed many cultures through developments such as the written word (cuneiform tablets), weatherproof buildings (bricks and roof tiles), sanitation and water reticulation (pipes) and, of course, art. The Terracotta Army of Xi'an, China, is a massive army of ceramic statues of warriors that was uncovered in 1974 by a farmer and dates back to 200 BCE. This incredible discovery is an example of how ceramics have helped us understand the economic and social history of that period, as well as the military hierarchy that existed at the time.

The oldest known fired ceramic piece in the world (so far!) is a tantalisingly small statuette of a nude female figure. It is just 11 centimetres high and filled with mystery – scholars are still debating its meaning. The Venus of Dolní Věstonice was discovered in 1925 in what we now know as the Czech Republic. Estimated to be about 30,000 years old, this ceramic sits alongside the oldest cave paintings of early modern humans.

Fast forward to the present and ponder the importance of ceramic material to our contemporary culture. What stories will our ceramics tell future generations? What will archaeologists of the future read into ceramics such as heat-resistant combustion engine parts? Or artificial bones and teeth? Or the tiles that clad our space shuttles? In the art history of the future, will Grayson Perry's ceramic vessels tell a proud story of changing cultural acceptance? Will Juz Kitson's sculptures claim a place using the historically understood purity of porcelain in new ways? Perhaps ceramics as a fashion accessory will tell stories of our obsession with the domestic home. While we can't know which stories will survive, in all likelihood our history will be evident for future generations in the ceramics of today.

Or will it? The partnership between clay and humans is an enormous privilege that comes with responsibility. The seemingly benign activity of making objects with clay and turning them into ceramics has important environmental consequences. From mining clay and associated ceramics materials, the embedded energy in transporting those materials, excessive use of water and fossil fuels and the polluting fumes emitted by kilns, to the waste created in the making process and the number of seconds (defective ceramics) discarded, our activities as ceramicists contribute to environmental degradation. The current explosion in popularity of making ceramics as a pastime raises serious questions about sustainability. There's no denying that in the Anthropocene epoch, we must make some changes.

Thankfully, we can do better. For example, it is now possible to ditch fossil fuels and fire kilns with 100 per cent renewable energy. And industry is already creating a circular economy for ceramic products and the waste that is created in the making process. Students can be encouraged to practice for a long time, repeatedly recycling their clay until they have found a strong direction for their work. As for end users, they can apply pressure by asking if materials are sourced locally and have a circular life. There are rich discussions to be had between suppliers, makers and consumers. Together we can learn and evolve new ways to reduce the impact of our activities while retaining and contributing to the cultural capital we leave behind for thousands of years to come.

JANE SAWYER

Jane Sawyer (janesawyer.com.au) is a ceramic artist and founder of Slow Clay Centre (slowclay.com), a ceramics education centre in Melbourne, Victoria. She is a member of the International Academy of Ceramics and has held board positions with Craft Victoria and World Crafts Council – Australia.

Previous: The work of Amy Leeworthy (p. 183).

Opposite: Ray Cavill's pottery wheel in use (p. 153).

The language of clay

Stephanie Outridge Field

People across time and place have connected through ceramics, and it has become their common language. It is a visual and experiential way of communicating and can be anything from child's play to the closest thing we get to real-life alchemy. Many cultures have used clay to tell their stories and document their lives and activities. But it has also been part of their economy, their rituals and ceremonies, their games and toys, their talismans and amulets – their very existence is informed and framed by ceramics.

The location of clay deposits, mainly found in places where watercourses slowed to deposit clay particles, are also often the sites where humans first gathered and established communities. Clay was an accessible medium that was an integral part of their lives, their culture and their identity. Humanity and ceramics have a shared history and many interconnecting stories create the rich brocade of that partnership.

What makes clay 'clay' is also what makes it a universal material. Clay is the result of the natural processes of erosion on the planet, whether by water, wind or ice. It can be used in many different states and forms, which encourages continued exploration and development. The philosophy of ceramics is the same. The philosophies surrounding the materials, the makers and the objects and their uses are worthy of investigation and continuing exploration.

Clay has also given us physical protection. We walk on it, we are housed by it and it populates our domestic and public environments. Clay is the basis of the roofs, walls and floors of dwellings in the past, in the present and, likely, into our future, thanks to contemporary ceramic technologies.

The Queensland Museum once displayed a large ovoid clay pot that had a small opening, about the size of a hand, that allowed access into the void. The pot was a soft pink-brown in colour, and had a thin rim with an exceptionally smooth, fine-grained surface. It was over 5000 years old. If you looked closely at it, you could see a thumbprint with distinct concentric lines. Immediately you connected with the maker through this very personal and individual mark that had been left in an instant but lasted thousands of years.

A shard, which is sometimes all that remains of a clay work, is always a key to another place, culture, time and tradition. Shards have been found everywhere on the planet, except the ice caps. Clay takes millions of years to form from base rock and is unique in its geological context. The clay in a shard can be traced to its place of origin, long before it was made into a pot to be used or traded, telling us how far it travelled.

Clay is a living philosophy that morphs and changes with each maker, place and time. Every maker or collector has a personal story that reflects their own journey with ceramics. You learn to work with clay from other people in formal and informal situations – from group classes with a master to casual but essential conversations with other clay people. The strength of the oral tradition of ceramics has served us well for centuries – the master teaches the apprentice, the teacher instructs the student, the elder guides the junior, and our peers both learn from and teach and us. It is the way it has been and always will be.

Clay is the fingerprint of humanity.

STEPHANIE OUTRIDGE FIELD

Stephanie Outridge Field is a ceramicist and founding director of MAKERS GALLERY, Brisbane, Queensland. She is a maker, student, commentator and curator of ceramics, as well as an appreciator of clay as a material and its role in everyday life.

Previous: The work of Jo Norton (p. 57).
Below: A selection of Sandra Bowkett's tools, slips, images and clay (p. 157).
Opposite: Serena Pangestu working on a vessel (p. 75).

Kirsten Perry's work and studio (p. 133).

EARTH

THROW

Arcadia Scott

CLAY BODIES: speckled and white stoneware; white raku
SURFACE FINISHES: mixes own glazes to create pastels; oxides for natural colours
KILN TYPE: electric
FIRING TEMPERATURE/CONE: 1280°C/2336°F, cone 9–10

'Clay is my soulmate' is how **Arcadia Scott** describes her relationship with her work. She has hit a sweet spot in her design by making beautiful, simple, functional work. She almost solely sells her work wholesale and works with her retail clients to meet their needs and changing trends. While her designs are her creation, she is happy to discuss colour trends in fashion and homewares and can create to suit her buyers.

She works five days a week, sometimes more, in her warehouse studio, which runs like a well-oiled machine. The studio space was a welcome and necessary change to her making process when the orders outgrew her capacity to work from home. The pressure point came when she realised her house had turned into more of a work space – her wheel was in the lounge room, a spare bedroom was used as a drying room, and she would glaze her work in the kitchen. Only the kiln, out in her shed, was not impeding on her living space. For two and a half years she worked in her home to keep outgoings low and allow her business to grow without the stress of high rental costs.

In 2020, she moved into her current studio. With 150 square metres to work in, she now has everything under one roof and her home is back to normal. The space has changed her approach to work. She feels more liberated about her practice and she attributes this to the space and openness of her studio. It allows her to make larger pieces, and everything has a place and purpose in the making process.

Arcadia's practice is centred around throwing. She is an early starter, and most mornings she is in the studio making by 7.30 am. A typical cup-making process is to throw about 120 cups on day one, then on day two, she trims and adds her fluting designs and handles while the clay is still slightly damp. The cups then dry for a week before a bisque firing. Next, she glazes and fires, then completes the last stages of sanding and finishing, packing and sending. Such a long process requires a good set of procedures. Arcadia's system needs to be accurate to ensure the orders are fulfilled as placed.

There are two or three batches of work going through the studio – cups, planters and tableware all on the go at any one time. Her output is almost production-level, but she achieves it mostly on her own. She does have help with glazing, sanding of the finished work, packing the orders and keeping the studio organised, so she can continue to design and throw each piece.

Arcadia has developed her own fluting design, using a loop tool to carve the clay. She then combines a base glaze with her chosen colour for that design. The combination of the fluting and glaze colours is how she achieves her unique overall style and creates ranges that are both collectable and can be mixed in with people's existing tableware. She favours glazes that give the finished piece a soft, satin feel – something she aims for in her glaze recipes. Her approach to colour is also a result of her being a painter, and the importance of colour comes through strongly in her work. Equally, the form and balance of a piece is crucial in her design. She is developing her range of tableware with functional and beautiful sharing plates and platters.

When she has downtime, she tests different clays and creates more test glazes, always thinking ahead, watching new trends and reacting to them. Arcadia's aim is to give the market what it wants but also to make work that is unique, collectable and never boring.

Above: Arcadia's process of throwing and carving.

Right: Test tiles are used to check how glazes will appear after firing.

EARTH — THROW

Asuka Mew

CLAY BODIES: stoneware mixed with wild clay from Dja Dja Wurrung Country (Trentham, Victoria)

SURFACE FINISHES: mixes commercial raw materials with natural oxides, wood ash, wild clay and rocks

KILN TYPE: gas

FIRING TEMPERATURE/CONE: cone 9–11

Asuka Mew is the maker behind Wingnut and Co. Asuka is originally from Fukuoka in the north of Kyushu Island, Japan, and his work has a strong Japanese aesthetic. When comparing pottery to painting, the artform he had earlier studied, he saw it as a refreshing change to make something beautiful and useful.

'As a child, I remember drinking tea with my family from a porcelain *yunomi* by Genemon. I would always choose the same cup. It had circles of cobalt brushwork repeated around the translucent vessel in columns of three. Each inky border contained five blue dots, reminding me of a lotus root or the segment of a persimmon.'

Asuka and his partner, Anna Miller-Yeaman, had a studio in the city for five years until 2020. They moved to Trentham in country Victoria between lockdowns during the Covid-19 pandemic. In their new country life they operate as sustainably as possible. Solar is their only source of power. On the many foggy or cloudy days, they are more reliant on heat from the fireplace in the house and a backup generator. Living sustainably is a mindset that spreads across their life and business and they know it will take time to be fully set up, doing it with as little impact on the world as possible. Asuka's current studio is in an old stable, where he throws work off a kick wheel and dries his pots next to a wood heater. He is building a purpose-made studio on the property and a woodfired kiln.

As well as being a painter and a potter, Asuka is also a furniture maker and woodworker and he employs all his skills in his daily pottery work. Some pieces have wooden lids or handles that he makes with timber he has milled from local trees that have fallen during storms. He is keen to make pieces with a combination of natural materials.

Asuka throws styles from his Japanese heritage, such as teacups, serving dishes and small plates. He says he likes the plate to complement the food, rather than be 'too noisy'. He has made a conscious decision to keep the designs consistent, so he can replicate and replace pieces in his collectors' tableware sets. With his range of vases, he prefers to work on different shapes. Asuka makes most of his work on the wheel and considers his practice production pottery. He relishes both the physical and repetitive nature of this kind of work. It suits him well.

His design work is minimal as he prefers to display the material of the clay, allowing the pieces to show the natural texture and colour. He digs white clay from a friend's dam and found iron-rich clay when digging his own vegetable garden. He combines groggy clays and finer clays and experiments with his own glaze tests. He enjoys learning about glaze chemistry, and it is an important part of his practice. Some of his best days are opening a kiln with test pieces to see if a piece he's been designing for a long time has worked out well.

Asuka would like to make pottery for a long time – as long as his body will keep up. He has chosen a path that is very physical at every stage, but ultimately rewarding, knowing that he has a hand in bringing the clay from the earth to create pieces that are timeless and have great functionality.

Previous: Pouring out excess glaze that has been used for the inside of a pot.

Above: Asuka's collection of glaze test tiles.

Right: Painting the porcelain using the shellac resist technique, which creates a raised effect and helps emphasise patterns and markings.

EARTH — THROW

Above: Carrying a ware board into the kiln room. Ware boards are used to carefully transport pottery from the wheel, minimising direct handling of the ceramics after they have been completed.

Opposite: Ceramics that are ready to be unloaded after a bisque firing – the first firing before any glaze is added.

Bridget Bodenham

CLAY BODIES: white raku; porcelain; stoneware
SURFACE FINISHES: clear glazes; mixes own oxides and stains; gold and silver lustre
KILN TYPE: gas
FIRING TEMPERATURE/CONE: 1280°C/2336°F with reduction at 900°C/1652°F

Creativity is in **Bridget Bodenham**'s blood. Her mother, Madeleine, is an artist and conservator of talent and skill across a range of mediums, and her father, Roger, was a sculptor and artist. One of her earliest memories of clay is watching her father sculpt clay busts of his children, which were later cast in bronze. Clay has always been her greatest love and her life's pursuit.

Bridget designed and built her dream studio, which sits on her family's property near Daylesford, Victoria. The large open studio of 180 square metres holds stock for her online shop and includes an exhibition space, as well as a kitchenette and relaxation space. A second room houses the kiln. This area is also used for glazing and decorating as well as drying the work, making use of the heat her large gas kiln emits. The kiln is fired up to five times a week – she is a prolific artist.

Her key requirement when creating the studio was lots of natural light. The space has a ceiling height of 6 metres that captures the light that streams in through large windows and allows it to be held and dispersed beautifully. Bridget's wheel sits in front of large windows on the western side of the building, giving her a view of the bush and Mount Kooroocheang while she is throwing.

Most workdays start with loading or unloading the kiln before throwing on the wheel. Her brother, Will, is her studio assistant. He helps with tasks like wedging the clay and some slump and drape mould work. This allows Bridget to focus on her prodigious production on the wheel. Quantities and styles are planned ahead of time so the production early on in the day can maximise both the bright morning light and Bridget's energy.

The afternoon is spent finishing – attaching handles, accents, feet or pearls to the morning's output. Once this is finished, Bridget moves on to administration and packing orders. Her routine changes depending on what kind of amazing work she is dreaming up. Her range is everchanging and includes everyday items such as cups, bowls and plates, but she also creates lidded vessels, cake stands, vases, soy pots, tea canisters, sake sets… the list is seemingly endless.

Bridget's distinctive decorating style is a deliberate response to the forms she creates, and she already has decorative ideas in her mind as she makes the raw form. She uses bold, graphic stripes, spots and blushes of colour in a restrained colour palette of pink, green and orange as well as cobalt and red iron oxides. She takes great satisfaction in creating the seemingly loose and gestural marks that she applies with brushes or foam brush applicators. Using these tools allows a lot of 'ink', so it allows her to keep her mark making fluid and intuitive, although deliberate. She is known for her splashes, dots and accents of gold and silver lustre, but her designs have evolved over the years. However, these marks maintain a thread that connects her work through the last decade and a half.

To honour the natural material of the clay, Bridget doesn't always fully cover the forms with colours or glaze. She thinks carefully about every step of the process, showing restraint if needed, so the proportions and structure of the final piece are celebrated.

Bridget continually comes up with new designs and loves the idea of making works that are both beautiful and useful. Her ultimate reward is creating works that her collectors get to interact with, be it putting flowers in a vase, presenting a cake on a stand or enjoying a comforting cup of tea. She is always inspired by the way people display food in their home and she reflects on this when creating a collection. Her friend Miriam has been a big influence in the playful presentation of food and has informed some of Bridget's ideas about pushing the limits of domestic design.

Opposite: Bridget handbuilding a crown sculpture.

Bridget's desire is to make work that allows people to appreciate the exchange of energy between themselves and the vessels they use in their daily life. For her, this is paramount in the pursuit of her life's work. The act of creation, not just the finished product, is what brings her most joy.

Opposite, clockwise from top left: Wedging the clay to remove any air bubbles or pockets; forming the clay using a pottery wheel; firing the clay to create ceramics; drying the wares to prevent any cracking or breaking in the kiln.

Hayley A. West

CLAY BODIES: ironstone; buff raku; red terracotta; stoneware; white powdered porcelain
SURFACE FINISHES: mixes own glazes, oxides and stains
KILN TYPE: electric
FIRING TEMPERATURE/CONE: 1100°C/2012°F for earthenware, 1300°C/2372°F for stoneware and porcelain

To calm and distract her active inner critic, **Hayley A. West** often listens to podcasts while making. The listening helps her escape and lets her instinct and muscle memory take over. She is a sensitive soul who is fascinated by how humans interact; her mind is filled with abstract thoughts of making forms. This means her works are not always practical, but often rather sculptural, telling stories in shape and form. Though functional work does interest her, it doesn't fit into her exhibition work and daily practice, so she only occasionally makes runs of plates and cups if commissioned.

Hayley grew up in a country town in New South Wales, but left to study at the College of Fine Arts in Sydney. She wasn't sure where to go with her art career and says she 'fell into ceramics'. It is the clay, she says, that has helped her heal. She studied interior and spacial design after her fine arts degree and this informs her ceramic work. She creates pieces while thinking of their relationship to the larger spaces in which they will be placed.

As a single mother and potter of nearly nine years, her normal working day starts after her two kids head off to school. She begins with cleaning and assessing what needs to be done in her ceramic studio that day. Hayley also teaches teenagers in her home-based studio, Wells Street Studio, in Sydney. Teaching is what she loves most, and it provides the income to support her exhibition practice.

Her backyard studio has five wheels, her kilns and an abundance of natural light. Many of her students have been coming to her for years because of the love of clay that Hayley has instilled in them. She prides herself on creating a safe learning and making space. She shares her own vulnerabilities with her students, allowing them to be themselves and freer on their clay journey. She also tells her students that the clay they use is a precious resource and they shouldn't expect to fire everything they create. She says learning and doing are as important as the finished work. She encourages her students to document their work by taking photos and to celebrate their finished pieces. Each piece is a future artefact, she says, and that is an amazing thing.

Hayley admits to not being an overly organised person, but she feels the discipline of ceramics keeps her in check. For larger forms, she starts with throwing and adds coiling on the wheel. She finds smaller works are meditative and easier on the body.

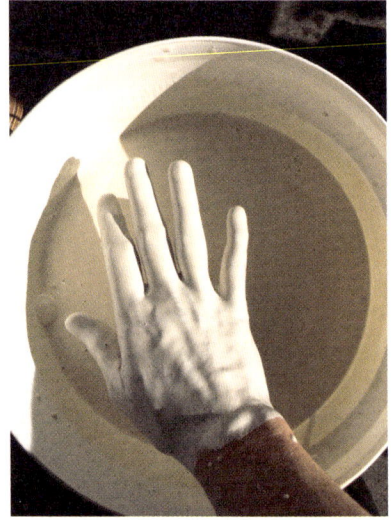

She credits her mentorship with Anthony Brink – a potter and teacher who has been working for forty years – for many of her glaze recipes. She achieves a large range of finishes thanks to her experience with Brink. Hayley produces stoneware and sometimes uses majolica as a base to give the colours a bolder finish. She oscillates between being quite serious and playful with the glaze application.

One of Hayley's signature styles is to create vignettes of two or more objects, playing with the space between and around them. These forms, and the tones of the glazes she uses, aim to portray the ephemeral nature of things. She believes that objects have souls and an unheard and unspoken existence; that they hold more than the simple forms they are; and that the motion, touch and interaction of the maker's hand in creating them gives them a value that is much more than they are often credited with.

Teaching and participating in exhibitions are the bulk of her practice. Although clay is her first love, Hayley is constantly thinking and adding ideas to her sketchbooks that explore other materials. She has a love of texture and is interested in incorporating the feel of materials such as fabric and weaving by making cords and strings.

A thoughtful and humble maker, Hayley understands clay, its limits and its beauty, and she celebrates all it gives to both the maker and the custodians of finished pieces. Most of all, as a teacher, she passes on this vulnerable, healing, earthy metaphor of the medium to her students.

Opposite, top to bottom: Combining clays; mixing glaze; wheel throwing.

EARTH — THROW

Jane Sawyer

CLAY BODIES: red earthenware; mixes own white slip
SURFACE FINISHES: mixes own terra sigillata, pigments and glazes
KILN TYPE: electric
FIRING TEMPERATURE/CONE: 1125°C/2057°F

Jane Sawyer has been a potter all her adult life. She can't remember a time when it wasn't part of her day-to-day existence. In the late 1970s, a craft train stopped at the country town where she lived. There was an artist in each carriage offering workshops, including one on raku ceramics and another on silver jewellery. 'I did the jewellery workshop and my sister did the raku. I was very jealous because she seemed to have much more fun! Someone should bring this concept back. I think it influenced me to choose a career in the arts.'

Jane trained as an art teacher before becoming a full-time potter in Melbourne. In her early ceramics career, she trained with Andrew Halford for three years. She credits Halford and his wife with encouraging her to travel to Japan, where some of her most profound training happened. She trained in the studio of the Shussai-gama Kiln in Izumo, Shimane Prefecture. There, where they practise the *mingei* philosophy – the idea that beauty can be found in functional, everyday objects – she had seven teachers. Jane produced work over and over and over to build up her skill. A deep respect for ceramics seeped into her making as she learned from these teachers with 'hand, head and heart all working together'.

Jane's studio is at her home in Melbourne. It was purpose-built in 2007, with drainage traps and a damp cupboard to slowly dry her sculptural and production work. She works up to seven days a week if she is preparing for an exhibition or a deadline. Before she starts on a new body of work, she usually has a week off and cleans down the studio for a fresh start.

She used to teach small classes at her studio, but when the waiting list had grown to 250 people, she opened Slow Clay Centre. The centre allows her to pass on her skills to more people but it also gives her and other artists the security of a regular day job that supports their artistic careers. This took the pressure off relying on selling her work.

Though Jane is a production potter by training, she felt it was becoming a grind and she wanted to explore her artforms more. She completed a master's in fine art at RMIT University in 2002, where she combined academic thinking with her making. This has seen her practice develop more conceptually. Jane now works on commissions and small batch commercial orders, but finds a satisfying balance by sharing her love of ceramics with the community through training and teaching while also focusing on her art practice through exhibiting.

Jane has stepped away from her use of wood and gas firing, where reduction and higher temperatures are the norm, and has electric kilns in her home studio. Her main clay is red earthenware (terracotta) and her signature work features her own slips, which she makes from dry ingredients. She fires to 1125°C/2057°F, and finds it still gives her the intended results but with the added benefits of being cheaper, quicker and easier. Slip goes on at the leather-hard stage of her forms and her distinctive way of mark making is to apply the slip with her hands, or by dipping, brushing, painting or sgraffito. Jane also likes the beautiful black clay she uses, as it is groggy and strong enough to stretch and re-form. However, she is most interested in slip, and although she uses oxides and stains occasionally to give the decoration more depth of colour, no matter the clay body, the addition of slip is where her work lands.

In her current work and thinking on clay, she is trying not to break down a piece into functional or sculptural, focusing instead on making 'a space' with the material. She feels that the clay has a relationship with her as the maker. Her hands might be doing something to create the piece, but the work still has its own existence. This is evident in her newer work, which is thrown on the wheel then draped, twisted and hung on purpose-made clay hooks as wall sculptures that reach their final shape in their residual fluidity in the kiln firing. This work shows the nature of clay and respects the base material, letting

Above: Putting freshly formed vessels into a damp cupboard.

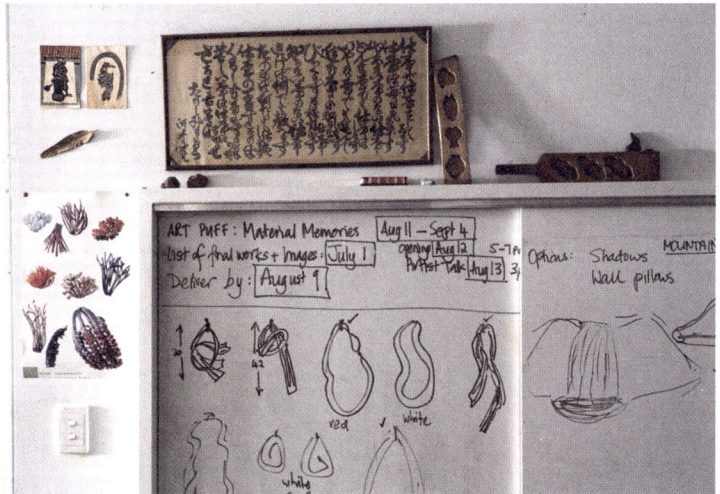 

it move almost on its own. What inspires her most is finding a new language in clay, not just trying to replicate what already exists, such as a classic Greek vessel or shape that has been replicated through the centuries. She wants to push and pull the boundaries and nuances of clay as a material.

    Jane is deeply interested in the environmental impact of ceramics and the thoughtfulness that must exist in conversations around clay as a medium. She explores and imparts this thinking with her teaching staff and students at Slow Clay Centre. She was pivotal in forming Clay Matters, a group that gathers to discuss environmental issues and publish on best practice in ceramics. Jane believes that objects can be a catalyst for connection between people and the story of her work, and her teaching continue to inspire the next generation of potters.

Above, clockwise from top left: Drafting design ideas; Jane working in the studio; altering a wheel thrown piece; compressing the clay.

Opposite: Studio corners.

Above: Finished pieces coated with slip and ready for the kiln.

Jo Norton

CLAY BODIES: stoneware; white raku; porcelain
SURFACE FINISHES: stain; slip; terra sigillata; clear underglaze
KILN TYPE: electric
FIRING TEMPERATURE/CONE: cone 6 or 8

Jo Norton thinks of her ceramics practice in three parts: everyday tableware, sculptural commissions and lifelong learning of a South Korean technique called *onggi*. She went full time with her practice in 2015 and now has a studio as part of an arts precinct, where she also has a gallery space. She is always happy to discuss her process and ceramics in general with anyone who drops by while she's working.

Jo's studio is on the Gold Coast in Queensland. She starts working early in the morning and generally begins by preparing clay and throwing through the first half of the day. She feels physically stronger in the morning and gets energy from throwing. Depending on the weather, she might work on the finishing in the afternoon, handbuilding, decorating and adding handles.

The tableware came to her first in her pottery journey. She is very aware of the importance of a vessel that is made for food, not only its style but, more importantly, how practical it is to use. She considers the shape of her wares, such as how the curve of a bowl is crucial to allow the spoon to follow the shape. Jo wants her work to be useful in all ways. Her coveted ceramic colanders have multiple serving and storage uses.

She thinks about the homes her work will go into and how they will stack in cupboards, but also how they can maintain a handmade aesthetic. To achieve that, she doesn't use a throwing guide, only weighs the clay to ensure the sizes will be similar and uses her eye as a guide.

Jo has had kitchen items that were invaluable to her over the years and that she has now recreated in clay. She started with an antique glass juicer that broke, which is now one of her favourite items to be recreated in clay.

Sculptural and larger works are increasingly capturing her interest and that of her customers. She is doing more hotel commissions and public art installations, and is keen for this to grow, as long as she does not lose her own voice in the work.

Jo visited South Korea a number of times and formed an interest in large fermenting pots. She has since returned to learn from one of the few teachers qualified in making these vessels. Onggi are large earthenware pots made for fermenting and storage. The building technique involves handbuilding with thick coils of earthenware iron-rich clay. While in Korea, she was struck by the notion that she was being gifted this experience and decided that she would spend time building on her knowledge and relationship with this unique process, and would continue learning this method with a master in Korea throughout her life. Jo says: 'When we learn something in Australia, we expect something to show for it.' Her experience in Korea was the opposite. The piece she was working on each day was broken down and the clay wedged again, ready for her to use in her learning the next day. 'The gift really is in the learning,' she says.

It's the feel of the clay that keeps her interested. That and the idea that with a bit of clay you can make something useful and beautiful. Sometimes the challenge is to focus on completing a body of work before starting with the next idea. Keeping things interesting by diversifying her body of work is a recipe for longevity, if only she had a bigger kiln.

Opposite, top: Vessels drying on the studio's shelves.

Opposite, bottom: Three vessels with three different clay bodies but the same surface finish.

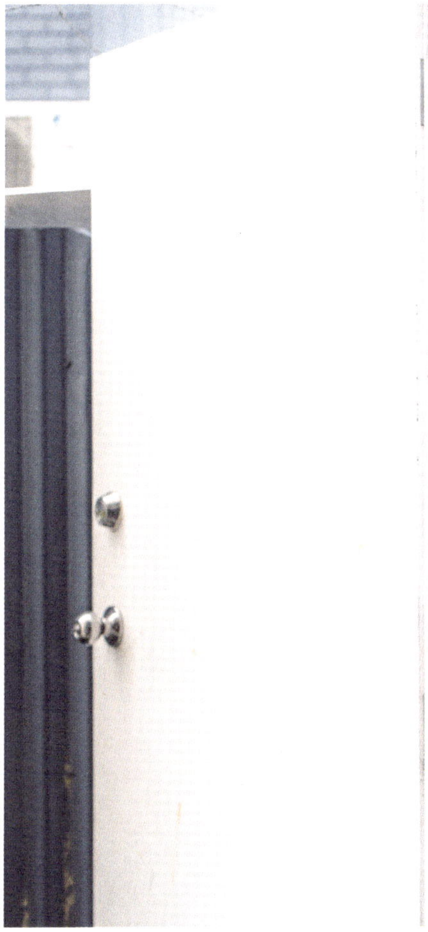

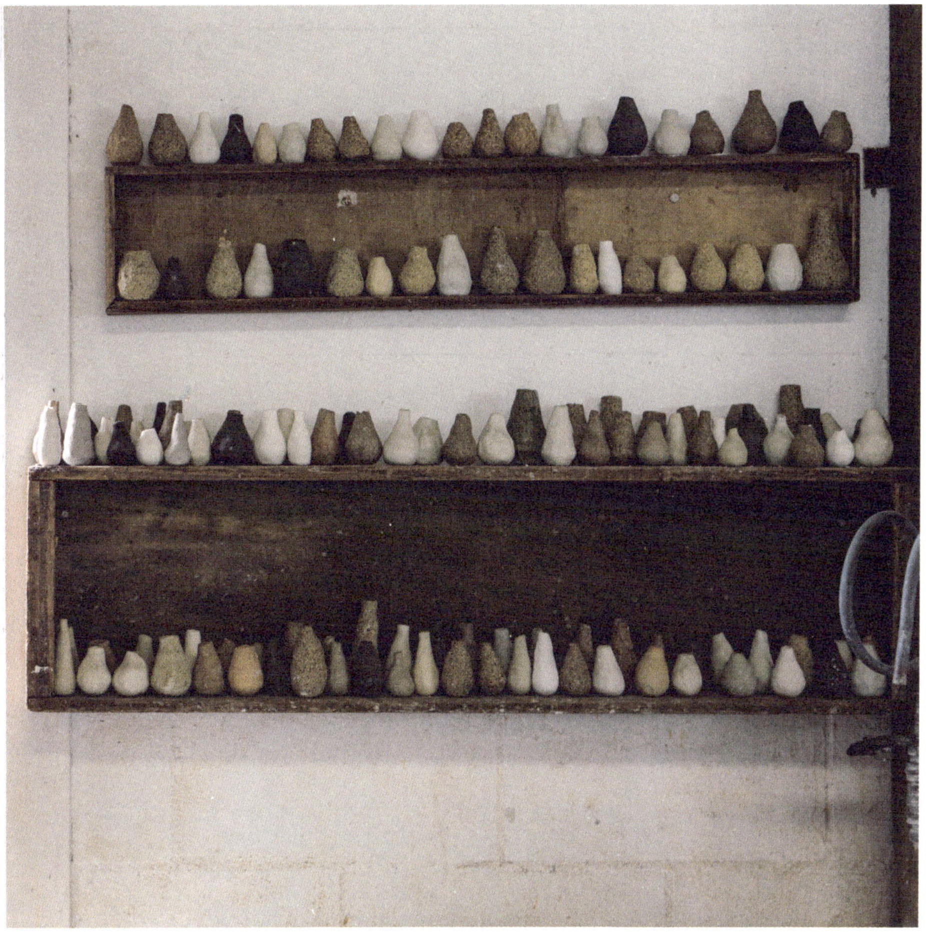

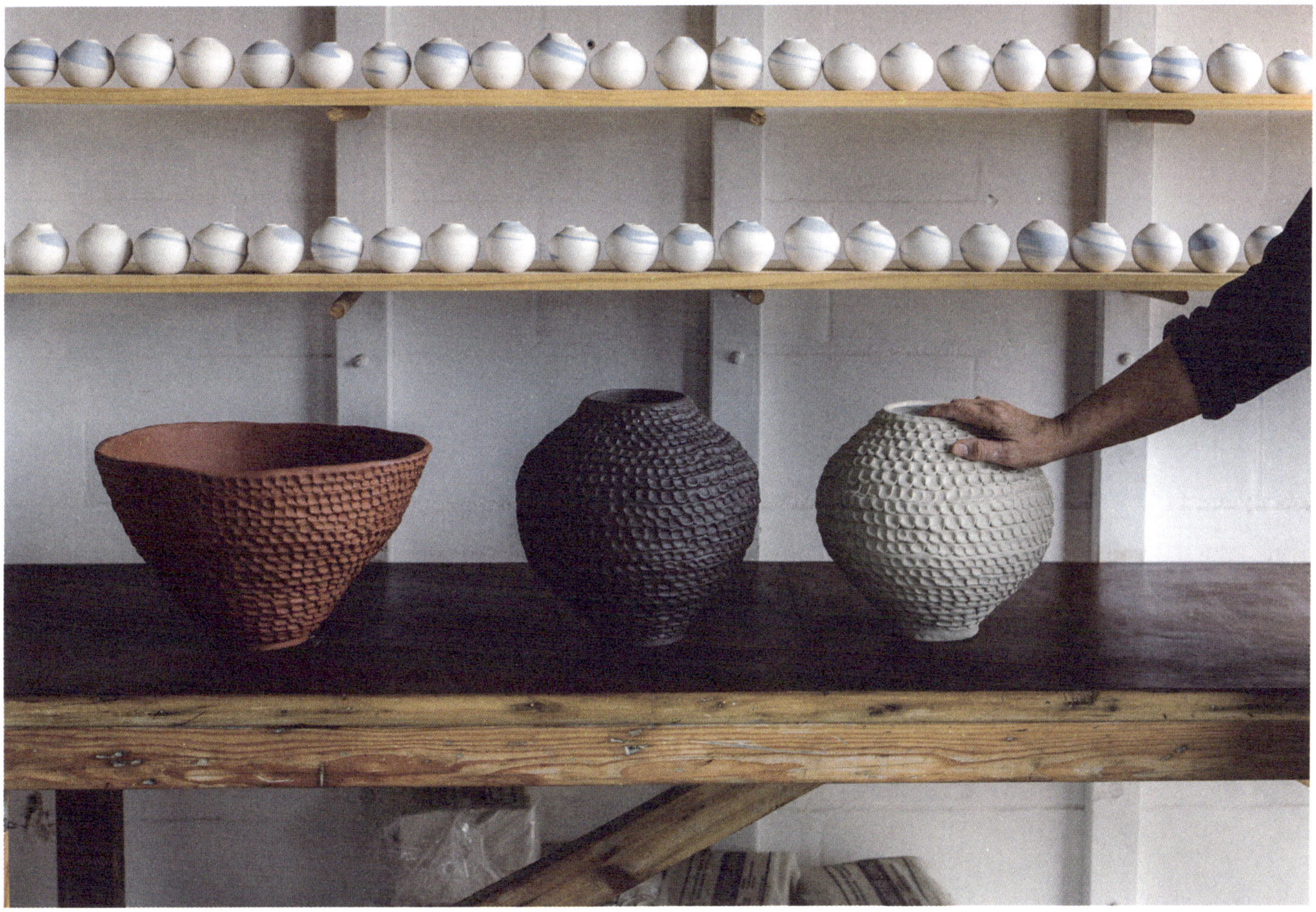

Kate Bowman

CLAY BODIES: mid-fire warm, chocolate and dark stoneware, and a recycled mix of all three
SURFACE FINISHES: various glazes, oxides and slips
KILN TYPE: electric
FIRING TEMPERATURE/CONE: 1255°C/2291°F, cone 7

Kate Bowman's mother was a potter and Kate first 'tasted' clay at the age of eleven, when she tagged along to one of her weekly workshops. 'Her teacher was an elderly Italian man who'd set up a studio at the back of his house. He'd just finished pulling bricks out of his old kiln. I remember thinking "You'd be mad to go to all this effort – it takes so long to cook!"'

Years later, Kate was working long hours as an advertising copywriter in Melbourne and felt completely burned out and in need of a change. Her husband, Steve, knowing her love of collecting ceramics, suggested doing a class. They lived close to Northcote Pottery, so in 2017 she signed up and took every workshop and course available. She also studied at the School of Clay and Art in Brunswick in 2019. Totally sold on the change to pottery, but balancing the need for income, she scaled down her copywriting work and built up her ceramic practice.

Part of developing her practice was understanding the type of pieces she wanted to make and how they would reflect her design style. Drawn to geometric shapes with a bold mid-century look, Kate pursued a process of inlaying clays to achieve this look. She soon found out this was not the easiest of methods. As one of her first large vases was fired, the shrinkage of one of the clays was greater than the other and pieces fell out of the inlay. She persevered and has since made some very successful pieces this way.

She has also found that darker textual clays and contrasting slips have produced a similar look with her designs. While sometimes the slip is added in painted or drip methods for more abstract work, Kate also uses resist methods with paper and wax to get bolder stylised shapes on her pieces.

The clay body Kate most prefers working with is dark stoneware. She uses a contrasting white matt clay slip as decoration, or a tonal dark stain to work in with the colour of the clay. With functional work, Kate produces a series so that a set of plates can be purchased together – each one is individual, yet they all come from the same batch. Seeing collections come together is very rewarding and something that Kate has become noted for. She is often approached to create a special series for a specific business. Between commissions, online sales and supplying stockists, Kate is working at capacity. She wants to pull back a bit so she can spend more time refining the work and testing new ideas.

As well as defining her pottery look, Kate focuses on functional ware – this forms the basis of her range. Vases, bowls, cups and plates that are sold individually or as sets are part of her regular output. Her studio is on the Mornington Peninsula, where she and Steve now live. They have created a multi-use space called Stoker Studio that houses her studio and is also available for hire as a gallery space, or for markets, workshops and events.

Kate splits her time between her own making, running the business, and teaching ceramics at Stoker Studio. Inspired by her own career change and love of clay, she wants to teach others and pass on her knowledge. Her biggest challenge now is finding time to dedicate to each area of the business and her own creative work in the studio.

Above: Test tiles for various inlays, glazes and slips.

Opposite: The stages of inlaying lighter clay into darker clay, with a finished piece bottom right.

EARTH — THROW

This page: A series of Kate's finished works.

Kate McKay

CLAY BODIES: ironstone
SURFACE FINISHES: mixes own glazes
KILN TYPE: gas and electric
FIRING TEMPERATURE/CONE: cone 10 with reduction

Kate McKay's studio is a 19th-century shearing shed constructed with hardwood slab and corrugated iron – a perfect ceramics studio. One of her earliest memories of ceramics is watching a family friend and acclaimed potter, Anders Ousback, building a woodfired kiln in her family's backyard. 'That backyard is now my backyard,' she says.

Kate studied ceramics at the Canberra School of Art, finishing in 1997, and has continued with her ceramics practice since. Most interested in functional wares, she is best known for her sets of stoneware plates, bowls and cups. She says that well-considered, handmade, functional tableware elevates the experience of shared meals.

She works at least three days a week in the studio at her home near Lake George in regional New South Wales, and the property and family take up the rest of her time. She tries to work those three days in a row to make the most of the momentum. On day one, she gets all the weighing of the clay done so she can come back on day two and get straight into making.

She mostly throws on a kick wheel, liking the meditative nature of the rhythm and the ability to work at a slower pace. She has her father's electric wheel as well, but finds that she has to concentrate on the piece too strongly. With the kick wheel, she says, there is a bit of distraction, so she doesn't over concentrate. She also just enjoys 'the honesty of the tradition'. Kate's signature is to leave the cutter's line – created as she removes the piece from the wheel – on the base of her work.

Kate's colour palette reflects the muted tones of a Morandi still life. She uses an ironstone clay for most of her work and makes her own glazes to keep the tones and texture consistent. Before glazing, she puts all the work through a bisque firing in the electric kiln, which goes on twice a month. Once all the work is glazed, which she does by dipping, she puts the gas kiln on to finish off the month's making cycle.

Kate is interested in doing more exhibition work with focused ideas, particularly around climate change and its impact on regional Australia, but will always make functional pottery. She enjoys knowing that the pieces she makes become part of the daily lives of others, of shared meals and cups of tea.

Clay will also remain her choice of material, as she has been involved with it since childhood, always chasing a perfect line or shape. She is in awe that with just earth and water and fire you can make something that is so useful to everyday life. It's the feel, the tactility of clay, and that it can offer both form and function. Kate is a maker at heart, she feels she can do what she wants to with clay more than anything else.

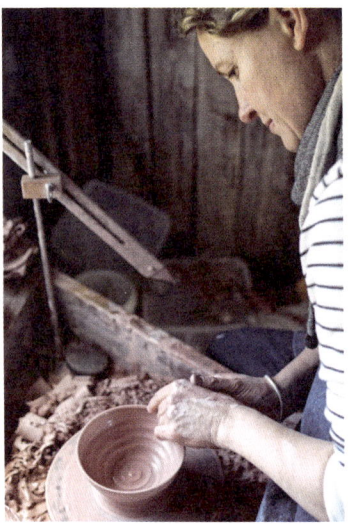

This page, top to bottom: A measuring tool is used for size consistency when making multiples of the same ware; wheel throwing using a kick wheel; a selection of Kate's clay tools.

Above: Cutter's line created when removing the piece from the wheel.

EARTH — THROW

Rebecca Lindemann

CLAY BODIES: fine white, warm and dark stoneware; porcelain
SURFACE FINISHES: mixes with base glazes of gloss, satin and matt, with different stains and oxides to create own range of colours
KILN TYPE: gas
FIRING TEMPERATURE/CONE: 1280°C/2336°F, cone 9

Rebecca Lindemann has been a potter for more than twenty-five years, since starting as a decorator at Yarra Glen Pottery in Brisbane in the 1990s. On seeing the process of throwing at the studio, she was intrigued by the possibilities of clay. Though she says she feels she 'fell into it', the conscious decision to put her hands into the clay changed the direction of her life. And she hasn't looked back.

She now lives at Mothar Mountain in Queensland, in a big house that she and her husband, Todd, transported here. They are raising their two children here and she works in a purpose-built studio just 20 metres from the house, next to her kiln shed. Todd built the studio using recycled doors and windows, timber and tin. The buildings rest in a clearing in the landscape. Rebecca describes the slope of the open space, which is framed by the Australian bush, as a curve that undulates like the sides of an upturned vessel.

Rebecca is in the studio most days, except Sunday. She loves that her ceramic practice allows her to be flexible to work around family time. Her main avenue for selling her work is the popular Eumundi Markets in Queensland, half an hour from her home, where she has had a stall for eleven years. Many customers return year after year, when they visit the area for their annual summer holidays. This honest and old-fashioned cycle of makers at markets and collectors visiting both delights her and sustains her work.

She spends the first week throwing and finishing, the second bisque firing, the third decorating, glazing and completing the final fire, and then repeats that cycle. In recent years, she has installed a pug mill to replace the arduous wedging of clay, and also to keep up the quality and quantity of work she is producing. She uses a mix of fresh and recycled clay and weighs up to four buckets of balls of clay to work through. 'Cups, cups, there are always lots of cups.'

Rebecca chooses to throw directly on bats. She has seventy-two that she cycles through in a day, in true production-potter style. Using bats means she does not have to cut each piece off the wheel as it is thrown. As well as cups, she makes jugs, vases and serving bowls. This also helps with heat distribution – in a kiln full of cups, some will warp, so she uses a variety of wares to accommodate the hot spots in the kiln.

She illustrates her work with Australian motifs. The family doesn't have pets, but a resident carpet snake lives between the roof of the house and her kiln shed, and when it's feeling cheeky it sometimes curls up in the corner of her studio when she is working. This snake has found its way onto her decorating palette and joins the magpies and native flowers that adorn her work. Rebecca loves creating useful and practical pieces, and although the illustrations she uses are popular with her collectors and she is passionate about the wildlife and flowers she depicts, she prefers a clean palette for her home and the day-to-day plates she uses with her family. Her previous decorating styles, when she had a city life, were fabric-like pattern designs she silk-screened on the vessels. Her new work is very representative of her surroundings.

Selling her work at the markets means she doesn't have to sell online or wholesale. The weekly markets and larger, twice-yearly markets she attends in Brisbane provide enough income. She loves the face-to-face aspect of markets and adores talking to people, hearing their stories and having communication spark over ceramics. She says she has a nice balance between hiding away in the studio and talking to customers directly.

Rebecca prefers to keep her shapes simple to ensure the functionality of the piece. She also adds a fingermark or dent to ensure that, despite her years spent perfecting a cup or bowl, it still has a small human mark to show that it is handmade. Though the time constraints of producing work for regular

Above: Rebecca using a pottery wheel to create her clay forms.

Opposite, top right: Painting motifs onto greenware with underglaze. Greenware is a term used to describe pottery that has been shaped but not yet fired.

markets doesn't allow much time for experimenting, she still works on the occasional piece outside the production realm, particularly new surface designs, which are important for providing her ongoing customers with something new to collect.

Rebecca loves her romantic potter's lifestyle. Her life fits around her practice and she carves out enough time for her family and a happy life in the bush. She finds the process of making relaxing, and although she works hard it doesn't consume her life. Being her own boss and living a chilled-out mountain life throwing pots is her idea of happiness.

Serena Pangestu and Anika Kalotay

CLAY BODIES: fine white, warm and dark stoneware; buff raku; porcelain
SURFACE FINISHES: satin white, yellow-brown matt and tenmoku glazes
KILN TYPE: electric
FIRING TEMPERATURE/CONE: 1260°C/2300°F, cone 9

This creative and pragmatic duo, Serena Pangestu and Anika Kalotay met at school and both completed undergraduate and master's degrees in architecture. Their studies gave them a good understanding of space, ergonomics and how good design can have a positive impact on people's lives, but they also knew that they did not want to work in an architecture firm. A ceramics course at the Fremantle Arts Centre led them to become the co-owners, designers and makers of Kura Studio.

Serena was born in Indonesia and moved to Australia when she was four years old. Her father has a deep interest in and appreciation for traditional South-East Asian arts and crafts. He has a small Chinese teapot collection and Serena vividly remembers him teaching her the difference between a high-quality and low-quality teapot. Anika's grandmother painted intricate designs on decorative plates, inspired by Hungarian folk art.

The word 'kura' comes from the Indonesian word for tortoise. They chose it as their business name because it was indicative of how they wanted to work. 'A tortoise moves slowly because it doesn't need to move fast.' Serena and Anika have been to Indonesia together many times and have spent time visiting local makers, from stone masons to textile weavers, iron casters and wood carvers. As they travelled village to village, they asked to observe the skilled locals at their craft, absorbing the knowledge of process and function as it has been done for centuries. They also understood that lifestyle and work can intertwine.

Serena and Anika knew they were designers and had found clay as their medium of choice. They knew that before making an object they must understand the processes it takes to get there. In 2017, they started Kura Studio with a collection of basic pieces that were useful but also thoughtfully made.

They found their individual strengths in the making processes. Serena is the wheel thrower and Anika does the finishing, handbuilding, glazing and firing. Though these roles are divided, they are on the same page when it comes to how the business runs, what directions they want to take and what designs they want to explore.

Their process is always different, each of them coming up with ideas. Sometimes the ideas are highly considered and drawn out, prototypes made and tested. Sometimes they are more sculptural works that come from their need for expressive creation. Their core range of household items, though, comes from seeing what doesn't exist locally but is highly useful in another country, such as their garlic graters and oil dispensers. Form and function are the most important goals for any piece they make. They take the time to work out the best placement of a handle or ledge for holding a piece. They find it fascinating and challenging to work out how a vessel will be used, how it pours, or holds the contents within its walls.

Their range of wares continues to grow, but the items that their collectors can't get enough of are their ever-popular ginger graters and incense holders. Both items are practical and beautiful, and this is exactly how they want their work to be used and loved. They love seeing how their work is enjoyed by their collectors and how it fits into their lives.

They are currently exploring larger sculptural forms, and see the freedom of breaking out of the production cycle of their practice as an exciting development. These sculptural works are also about giving them both time to explore and see the limitations and breadth of clay as a material. Harking back to their architectural and spacial training, this new direction shows their talent and desire for experimental leanings.

Above: Serena Pangestu (left) and Anika Kalotay (right).

Their special bond gives these women the freedom to exist in each other's creative work. It is often said it is hard to work with friends, but these two defy that. Finding and working to their individual strengths and weaknesses is the key to the success of Kura Studio. But more than the daily work they do together, it is their strong belief in good design and their thoughtfully made work that are central to their happiness.

Opposite, left: Turning to create a foot on the vessel – done when the piece is at leather-hard stage but needs trimming, and is usually completed on the wheel.

Above, right: Compressing the handle of the cup into the body.

HAND

Anna Scheen

CLAY BODIES: stoneware; white raku; porcelain
SURFACE FINISHES: commercial glazes, but mostly left unglazed
KILN TYPE: electric
FIRING TEMPERATURE/CONE: 1280–1300°C/2336–2372°F

Anna Scheen is both a dedicated painter and ceramic artist, but her studio space is solely for clay work, as she prefers to paint in the house in the evenings. Despite this separation, each of her practices informs the other.

In 2001, Anna moved to the Macedon Ranges, Victoria, into a little cottage on one-third of an acre, where she worked in a spare room. In 2007, she set up her first studio in the garden shed. In 2020, she converted her two-car garage into a bigger studio and a gallery space open to visitors.

Her new studio is a very connective space, linking her to her work, her garden and the customers who visit. It was important to capture the natural rural light when repurposing the garage, and clear roof panels and white-painted walls help achieve that. Anna is a dedicated worker and starts with her coffee in the studio every morning, getting a feel for what has to be done that day. She is also a self-admitted daydreamer, so this time is occasionally spent gazing at the garden and thinking about the forms or characters she will resolve in clay that day.

Anna generally gets the admin of running her own studio out of the way in the morning, tidying her space, emailing and filling online store orders. By around 2 pm, she hits her stride and the clay work takes over. She can focus on the clay without distraction and loses herself in the making.

Her sculptural work is intuitively made; when she begins creating a form, she doesn't know how it will end up. No drawings, no preconceived thoughts about how it will resolve, just hands in clay and her artistry taking over. She starts by cutting down the clay and plays until the piece reveals itself to her. For the most part, she knows instinctively when the piece is finished and when to stop. Sometimes, if the piece is not coming together, she pushes through the instinct to stop and start again, and is able to turn it around, the form taking shape even if it is a completely unexpected one.

The thing Anna loves most about clay is that it suits her building process. There is no other material that she can add to and take away from with such flexibility. Given how organically her sculptures come into existence, this makes complete sense. The colour of the clay is crucial to Anna, and she chooses to work with a white raku for handbuilding forms. When the clay is leather-hard, she uses imperial porcelain slip to get a stark white finish. She then starts by lightly mapping out a design before painting using underglazes. Her palette is quite limited and often monochromatic, with the focus on the contrast between the white clay and black underglaze. Black, her favourite colour, is used consistently and is sometimes accentuated with one or two other colours. Her work has an intentionally quiet nature.

Her functional wares are also designed with underglaze and a steady hand. Her very popular gin cups are created from imperial porcelain and are made very fine – the finished cups are almost translucent. Not easily achieved, this is like seeing into a world that is otherwise hidden. The designs on the outside are somewhat visible from the inside of the vessel. Anna's intention is clearly to give the user of the piece a view from an alternative perspective. To experience this is quite special.

Anna loves the finished work more than any other stage. This is when the secrets of the designs and clay merge to show exactly what she intended. The emotion of the work comes through and the abstract mark of a brush can produce the best outcome. It's also why she doesn't repeat work; each piece she makes is unique in shape and design. This uniqueness is why her pieces resonate with people, and hearing the stories of her buyers is where Anna finds the most joy in her artful life.

Previous: Painting onto the vessel using underglaze.

Bonnie Hislop

CLAY BODIES: fine white stoneware; light and dark mid-fire speckle
SURFACE FINISHES: underglaze colours with clear glaze over the top; gold and silver lustre
KILN TYPE: electric
FIRING TEMPERATURE/CONE: 1220°C/2228°F, 700°C/1292°F lustre

Bonnie Hislop is a romantic at heart. She lives with her heart on her sleeve and, while she would love romance to be central to her life, she knows that life is hard, relationships are hard and being a woman is hard. Bonnie has found her voice and is using it loudly through her work. Now in her mid-thirties, she wants to speak to her generation and is doing that through the messages on her vessels, which are earning her attention.

Bonnie has been drawing her whole life and has been around clay since she was eight years old. Her mother, Karen, is also a ceramicist and Bonnie made small jewellery pieces with decorated faces and doll pendants when she was young. It was a medium that always held her interest but she didn't consider it a career option, instead working in theatre, fashion, communications and publicity. But she still worked with clay alongside her illustration, so it was inevitable that the two would combine. She decided that if she was going to be a full-time artist, she needed to get much better at her art and develop business skills.

Bonnie's '10,000 hours' mostly came from making highly illustrative cat cups and planters. The repetitive forms and illustrations honed her skills and she found the clays, glazes and tools that she would continue to work with.

Now the owner of Dabbler Studio in Brisbane, which is also the home of Bonnie Hislop Ceramics, she has carved out a business of workshops and open studio nights, alongside her own artistry and exhibition work. For the past few years, she has been working pretty much seven days a week. Her mother works on glazing and firing in the studio, and an assistant, Michelle, helps build a range of retail forms for Bonnie to illustrate. The retail range and workshops allow Bonnie time and quiet to work on her art pieces.

Her art pieces are exaggerated and flamboyant and all handbuilt. She uses bright colours and metallic finishes to cover the surface of her vessels. To achieve these bright colours, she does a bright white underglaze on the bisque form, then sketches over that with details in pencil before painting on the underglaze colours, working from lightest to darkest. If there's a lustre finish, that is painted on after the mid-fire and the piece is fired a third time just for the lustre.

Bonnie's other impetus is owning her own voice. This has come with time and maturity and a belief that her voice is as important as anyone else's. When she started using her artwork to speak her truths, she had to become braver than ever before to put them out into the world. It's a source of both anxiety and excitement to put her words on her work but it's a challenge she's up for, especially since she has found an audience who wants to hear what she has to say. She wants her work to be a balance of joy and her thoughts on the human experience.

Bonnie's messages are, for the most part, positive and affirming, particularly for women. But there are many layers within the work. She mostly works on her art pieces when the studio doors close and she can get to a place of deep focus and quiet. With so much fine line work to do, she needs the quiet to decompress and achieve the best outcomes. So far, she hasn't had trouble pulling ideas together. With so many running through her head, she usually quickly sketches out her thoughts so she can clear her mind and come back to them later – 'or never', she jokes.

The bigger her vessels get, the bigger the risk that firings won't be successful, but she loves the magic of the medium, especially because you never have full control over it. She calls it a partnership that requires respect or 'listening with your hands'. She understands she will only ever have so much say in how it comes together, but that is exactly where she finds the pockets of romance and magic.

Previous: Sponging back the sides of the vessel to make it smooth.

Above, top right: Painting using underglazes.

Above, middle right: An underglaze colour wheel test plate used to show what the underglazes will look like once glazed and fired.

Cara Edwards

CLAY BODIES: white stoneware; buff raku; red terracotta
SURFACE FINISHES: underglaze colours; clear or white gloss glaze
KILN TYPE: electric
FIRING TEMPERATURE/CONE: cone 5–6

Cara Edwards moved to Tasmania to pursue a lifestyle of local farming and horticulture and, along the way, she found pottery. She went to night classes to study ceramics as a way of meeting new people and to find a creative outlet in her new home state. Having previously studied and worked in graphic design, her sense of line and scale informs her organic handbuilt ceramics.

Cara returned to South Australia for a year to care for her terminally ill mother, and during this time she turned to clay daily. Working with the clay in her hands and experimenting with knowledge gained through an adult education pottery class was a salve during a sad time in her life. Her father found a cheap second-hand 1970s kiln in a neighbouring town and tinkered away, getting it into good condition for Cara to use. She worked at the kitchen table in their house, and after her mother died her father strapped the reconditioned kiln to his ute and transported it to her Tasmanian studio.

Her studio is in Charlotte Cove, in her father-in-law's home. The cold climate means she often wears thermals and ski jackets while her hands work in the chilly mud that is clay. From the studio, she can see the waters where the Huon River meets the sea in this rugged landscape. Cara and her partner, Fin, have built their own home, a tiny house in Deep Bay, 10 kilometres north of Charlotte Bay. They live a slow and thoughtful life, growing and preserving their own vegetables. In winter, their garden is less work and hiking is harder, so she works full time on her ceramics through winter.

Cara works weekdays in the studio, making her small handbuilt vessels, bells and jewellery pieces. Selling her work through markets and wholesale to retailers around Australia, Cara only fires twice a month – a bisque and another for a glaze firing. Between the two firings she decorates with underglazes, drawing reference mostly from patterns in nature. As her work is small, this is all that is needed to keep her practice ticking along. She has a six-week cycle making work, including drying time (often longer than in other climates). She likes the routine and cycle of the work, pairing shapes that match, decorating them, glazing and firing them. Because she uses a groggy clay base called BRT (Buff Raku Trachyte), there is also a considerable amount of sanding work.

She doesn't wholesale the vases and dishes, so this is where she can be extra creative and she feels this work enriches her collections. Most of her signature design and pattern work is created on top of a white base glaze, using colour glaze applied with a pen nib to get her fine lines. Cara continues her learning through information from the internet and YouTube videos. The science behind clay is not her strong point, but she is eager to learn. Her focus is on the mark making, not the technical side of glazes.

Cara's lifestyle is based on nature and living at one with it, so it is only natural that it is her greatest muse. She is both in awe of nature and inspired by it, and spends all her non-clay time in nature. She feels like it is Christmas Day every time she opens the kiln and although her work is selling to collectors around the country, she also has a local following of friends and farmers, and people who choose to wear her jewellery on special occasions. This slow and gentle practice and response suits her just fine.

Previous: Kiln shelves filled with bisque wares.

Opposite, top right: Cutting earring pieces from the clay.

Opposite, middle left: Hand pinching a vessel.

EARTH — HAND

95

Clare Unger

CLAY BODIES: speckled, warm and black stoneware; porcelain
SURFACE FINISHES: mixes own glazes; underglazes of white, cobalt, iron and manganese oxides
KILN TYPE: electric
FIRING TEMPERATURE/CONE: 1200°C/2192°F, cone 6

Clare Unger thinks about how the past influences the present, and she represents this in her ceramic work through the use of textiles and stitching patterns to mark her clay forms.

Clare is originally from Zimbabwe and studied fine art in Cape Town. Her parents had a collection of ceramics made by the British potter William Staite Murray, who was her father's great uncle, and her mother also collected traditional African pottery made by women potters from their local area in Zimbabwe. Clare moved to London in 1996 with her husband and began her study of ceramics there. When they moved to Sydney in 2001, she undertook a diploma and then an advanced diploma in ceramics.

Clare had a skirt that was her mother's, covered with applique that her mother had stitched, and she wanted to use that stitching to mark her clay. It was a way to continue the life of her mother's work, to mix the memories of things. She wanted the stitches to appear in the clay as they would on fabric – sitting out from the clay, rather than pressing into it. To achieve this embossed look, she created moulds by rolling the textile onto a slab of clay and then bisque fired it to become a mould. She then used the mould to create a hand-stitched look in slabs of clay that she makes into handbuilt vessels.

She works quickly, as she gets the best results when the clay isn't yet leather-hard. She cuts and moulds the embossed slabs to a shape, adding tucks and pleats and gathering the clay as if it was fabric. Once removed from the form mould, she continues to manipulate the clay to create the vessel's individual finish. She is a perfectionist by nature, so she spends time on the small details on each piece.

Her porcelain vessels are mostly functional homewares – teacups, spoons and bowls – and she says that both textiles and ceramics have a 'humble domestic' use, but she aims for a stylistic version of the mark rather than a literal one. Her palette is quiet. She chooses a more matt finish glaze overall. She works on developing glaze techniques to enhance the marks, such as painting the patterns with an oxide mixture of cobalt, manganese or iron so they appear grey or brown after the final fire. It's an ongoing experiment, but she is happy to continue as long as she feels she is moving forward.

Finding the balance of fine art with a vessel intended for everyday use can be a challenge for Clare. She likes to think about her work conceptually, and works that way, with the reason and resonance of the pieces being tied to another hand by using stitching. That those stitches originally came from her mother's hand and now exist on vessels made by hers gives them another life and a new story.

When Clare's mother died, she inherited the family art collection, things that give her a reminder of where she grew up and a connection back to her childhood. These connections to the past, the way they influence her today and how they will be considered in her future work will be her enduring legacy. Clare unfolds those memories and creates her work with them in mind. Creating the patterns in the way she does is time-consuming and exacting, but this yields a unique and tactile, yet calming, result.

Above: Marking a slab of clay.
Opposite: Using a handmade mould to emboss the clay.

EARTH — HAND

Hyeyoun Shin

CLAY BODIES: mid-fire porcelain; chocolate and dark stoneware
SURFACE FINISHES: underglaze colours; matt white glaze
KILN TYPE: electric
FIRING TEMPERATURE/CONE: 1220°C/2228°F, cone 6

Gold Coast potter **Hyeyoun Shin** grew up in Busan, a coastal city in South Korea. Her strongest memories of her school days are the rigid conformity that was imposed on the students. Today, her ceramic sculptures, especially those of tiny girls, reflect those memories but often with a nod to defiance or cheekiness – the same feelings she had back then.

These small sculptures, along with her wall pieces, give Hyeyoun a point of difference in her work. Korean houses are smaller and therefore so is the furniture and artworks within them. The small scale of her pieces doesn't seem unusual to her.

Hyeyoun long had a desire to learn ceramic art, but at art school she chose visual design as her field of study. The course focused on graphic design and product design, and these skills have been valuable in her ceramics. Much of the design work she studied was three-dimensional, so she can think and design that way regardless of the medium.

When Hyeyoun moved to Queensland with her husband, Joseph, she found her way to ceramics. She started classes at the Gold Coast Potters Association and immediately knew it was one of the best decisions of her life.

The aim of Hyeyoun's work is to produce functional and beautiful objects that can make a space feel like a home. Even the smallest of her sculptures can hold a dried flower or leaf. She loves that her work is completed by someone's interaction with it. Her wall pieces, all handbuilt, are most often a combination of different-sized vases sitting within a frame. The purchaser, by adding their own garden treasure, can create a still life of their own.

Her love of old furniture and animals comes through in her sculptures. Recreating furniture in miniature takes patience to get right, for drawers to open to reveal a book or pencil, for example. These pieces give Hyeyoun real joy to make. She moulds the clay by hand to shape various household items, or a cat sitting on the head of one of her girls. She always sketches out an idea before making it. If it doesn't work as a sketch, she knows it won't work as a sculpture. She trusts her design training and understanding the limits of the clay. Her preferred clays are porcelain or dark chocolate stoneware and she uses them to create contrast.

Much of the frame work is either left neutral or has only minimal design painted on with underglaze colours, allowing any additions to be made by the owner. Her girl sculptures, on the other hand, are where Hyeyoun plays with the design and brings them to life – some settle in reading a book quietly, another stands with arms crossed firmly in defiance, or has a knitted beanie pulled down on her head. Hyeyoun doesn't like to make the same thing multiple times – what she makes each time is unique and is often related to her feelings on the day.

Opposite, top left: Design ideas and paper patterns for vases.

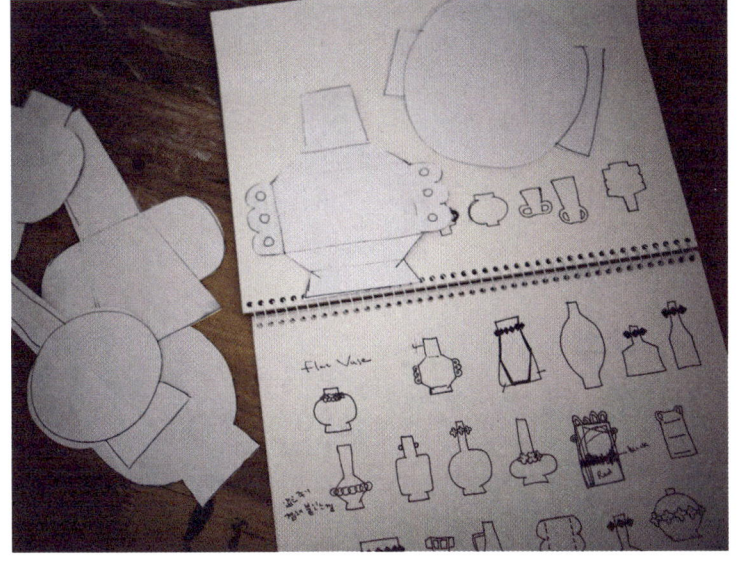

EARTH — HAND

103

Jennifer Orland

CLAY BODIES: white raku; terracotta
SURFACE FINISHES: white gloss glaze; lustre
KILN TYPE: electric
FIRING TEMPERATURE/CONE: tableware 1100–1130°C/2012–2066°F; vases 1280°C/2336°F

The natural world is the biggest inspiration in **Jennifer Orland's** work, in particular the undeniable beauty of Australian nature. One of the first floral motifs that Jennifer used in her work was Geraldton wax, which she still uses as a recurring theme on her pieces.

Jennifer has an affinity with the arts and crafts movement of the 1930s. It was a time when artists and makers turned to nature and the handmade to create work that stood out against mass-produced ceramics and domestic goods. Their pottery was full of florals and patterns and extreme design but, for Jennifer, it is the way that florals were stylised in Australia that is a source of inspiration for how she uses native plants in her work.

Jennifer has always been a painter and she studied theatre at university, but when she started a night course learning ceramics in early 2003, she found that making objects had a different reward. Building a piece of work from an idea and getting close to what she imagined was actually quite satisfying. She initially hired a wheel (which she eventually bought) and invested in a second-hand kiln, which she still uses. Most of her work is handbuilt now and she uses slabs and moulds to create her pieces.

She has a consistent range of tableware – plates, bowls and small dishes – where subtle rambling patterns of Australian native flowers sit in relief on the forms. These delicate designs are formed by carving into plaster moulds and draping and pressing the clay into them. The beauty of the designs is accentuated with the use of white raku stoneware clays and terracotta with a white glaze that highlights the relief patterns.

A fan of the great Australian artist Margaret Preston, Jennifer has a range of vases she calls the Preston Vases. These are a nod to Preston's woodblocks, and Jennifer frames relief carvings of flowers and plants within a solid wall of clay. While Preston's paintings and prints were often bold and bright, Jennifer keeps her palette to a soft white. She became hooked on relief carving when she was learning and it is what makes her work so tactile.

Because pressing the moulds into the clay requires a strong surface under the clay, she has a series of moulds that fit the shapes she works to. Jennifer also has smaller handmade plaster stamps that she uses to create freestyle patterns on the exterior of vessels. Her small but light-filled studio under her home in a Brisbane suburb houses her kiln, cupboards and shelves of clay, and her tools, books and moulds. She sells her work to stores and galleries and takes part in exhibitions from time to time. Her practice is considered and thoughtful – much like Jennifer herself.

Jennifer listens to her body and mind and works accordingly. If her energy isn't right, she listens to that and trusts that it will come back. Working from a studio at home allows her to be mindful in this way. When she's inspired, there isn't much that stops her working on her larger pieces. When she needs to ease off, she loses herself in repetitive work, like making her bluebird and bee brooches. Inspired by the ocean, she has recently been working with seashells, using them to give the clay natural impressions. Her greatest pleasure is observing details in nature, thinking about how that would translate into her work, and then seeing that come to fruition.

Opposite: Jennifer rolling out a slab of clay to impress with her handcarved relief tools.

Mel Eliades

CLAY BODIES: speckled, white, warm and dark stoneware; buff and white raku
SURFACE FINISHES: white satin glaze; underglaze colours; cobalt oxide wash; black, grey and white slip
KILN TYPE: electric
FIRING TEMPERATURE/CONE: 1220–1260°C/2228–2300°F

Mel Eliades is a relative newcomer to pottery, having only touched clay for the first time in 2017. But when she did, it was completely transformative, and there is true joy when she speaks about those first experiences and of every day since. She says she will be a potter until she's 'old and grey'.

Living in a regional Victorian town, she had few options for learning but she did classes at Made in Clay in nearby Wangaratta. The first course was in handbuilding, which she enjoyed immediately. The second was wheel throwing, which she found frustrating. She was consumed by the challenge and spent hours practising, then bought a wheel and kept teaching herself until she got it. She is mostly self-taught, attending workshops when she can, learning through trial and error and watching videos.

Mel has combined both techniques: wheel throwing to get the vessel's form started and handbuilding to add complexity to the design. Carving is her favourite form of design. She says she wasn't at all concerned about taking a carving tool to the clay, it felt natural and she loved seeing the transformation it can bring to a piece.

Her background in nature photography, macrophotography in particular, and an obsession with the blue-banded bee, led to her choice of business name. Clay Beehive was born. Today she spends much more time with clay than the camera, but the photography is crucial for selling online. Mel has converted an old garage on her property as her studio, lining the walls and adding a heater to keep the space workable through the colder days.

Mel plans her work in a fortnightly schedule. Once planned, she is focused and motivated to get the pieces made and uploaded for sale on her online shop. She currently has a smaller kiln than she'd like, but given where she lives and the cost to have three-phase electricity put in, she just fires more often.

Mel uses inspiration from her garden to create flourishes to her vessels that are reminiscent of flowers and grasses from her property. She also uses repetitive patterns from fabric designs. Much of Mel's work is everyday tableware, which she likes to make while imagining people using them. Functionality, in both size and weight, is important and she considers this as she makes each piece. Mel particularly likes making vases and vessels, as she allows herself to enjoy the motion of carving clay and the way it feels in her hands. She says the look is unplanned and simply a by-product of her enjoyment.

She is continually testing glazes in her studio, learning which colours work well with which clay bodies and which finish – gloss or matt. When she wants to keep the raw feel of the clay on a functional piece, she uses a silicon-based liquid ceramic sealant to seal the clay so it is food-safe. Mel is the kind of maker who just wants to get in and give it a go. If she can see something in her mind and imagine it as a three-dimensional piece, she will make it. Sometimes it works, sometimes it doesn't, but, to her, everything is a learning experience, and she is happy to keep learning.

Opposite, top right: Adding handbuilt flourishes to a wheelthrown vessel.

Roshni Senapati

CLAY BODIES: white porcelain
SURFACE FINISHES: own glaze mixes for white satin and matt; gold lustre
KILN TYPE: electric
FIRING TEMPERATURE/CONE: 1280°C/2336°F, cone 10

Roshni Senapati moved to Australia from Mumbai, India, in 1980 with her husband, Nik. Nik is a geologist, so they moved around every two or three years. As an early childhood teacher, Roshni could work anywhere, but constantly moving made it hard to keep up with her clay craft. At each new place, she set about making large handbuilt pots. That kept her hands in clay, and she could leave them behind when the next move happened.

In 2015, Roshni decided to stop working as an educator and concentrate on her work as a ceramicist. She enrolled in Brisbane's Clayschool where she honed her skills over five years while also working from her home studio in Paddington.

Roshni says handbuilding was the most enjoyable and natural practice for her. Her journey has focused on the message and concepts behind the work. Her Indian heritage and ancestral history, which didn't interest her when she was younger, has become central to the pieces she now makes. 'It all came to me at the right time, to understand and be interested in my history and culture.' This came through an experience of having a silk sari refurbished in New Delhi in 2008.

That sari, originally made in the 1960s, had real silver thread woven into its border. When she collected it, she was given a bag of the leftover silk remnants. In 2019, Stephanie Outridge Field, owner of Makers Gallery in Brisbane, asked her to be part of a show called *Threads*. Roshni started talking to her mother and researched her history to understand more about the sari fabrics. This helped her realise that memories are woven through time, like threads through a sari.

Roshni's Encircle series of porcelain vessels are made by wrapping rolled clay around a cardboard tube in a fluid motion, just as a sari is wrapped around a body. She takes the tube away when the clay is strong enough to hold its shape, so she can keep wrapping and create the base. At leather-hard stage, openings are made for the sari thread to sew fabric to the vessels later.

Once dry, the vessels are bisque fired. A specially mixed glaze creates a white satin finish inside the vessel, with a white matt glaze on the outside. It is crucial that glaze hasn't filled in the openings she will sew through, so she pushes a pin through all the openings again. She then spends a lot of time polishing the outside of the vessels, using wet and dry sandpaper, starting rough and progressing through finer sandpaper until the clay feels like silk in her hands.

For most ceramicists, there is little more to do once the glaze firing is done. But for Roshni, that is only the first half of the work completed. She spends a month creating a series of vessels, usually about thirty pieces. She cleans down her studio of her clay work and sets it up as a sewing space, then uses threads and fabrics to create the final pieces.

Roshni gives as much consideration and weight to the fabric as she does the clay work. Her journey with clay and fabric has been far more personal than she anticipated, opening up a history and culture that she hadn't spent much time investigating through her life. She now has a deeper connection to her mother through her stories of Indian culture and heritage – stories that have a new life through her work. Even the curved base of her works are a reference to the round-bodied water bottles that feature in her earliest memories of the India of her childhood. Her mother has enjoyed seeing Roshni combine sari fabrics and threads into her work, and has given her more of them to work with.

Roshni is touched that people are responding to the work because it is so personal for her. She didn't know if others would understand it or connect with it enough to want to take it home. They have, and Roshni's decision to tell her story through her work has helped other people find their story within it too.

Opposite, top left: Removing a strand of silk.

Opposite, top right: Sewing silk through the vessel.

Opposite, middle left: Glazing the inside of the vessel.

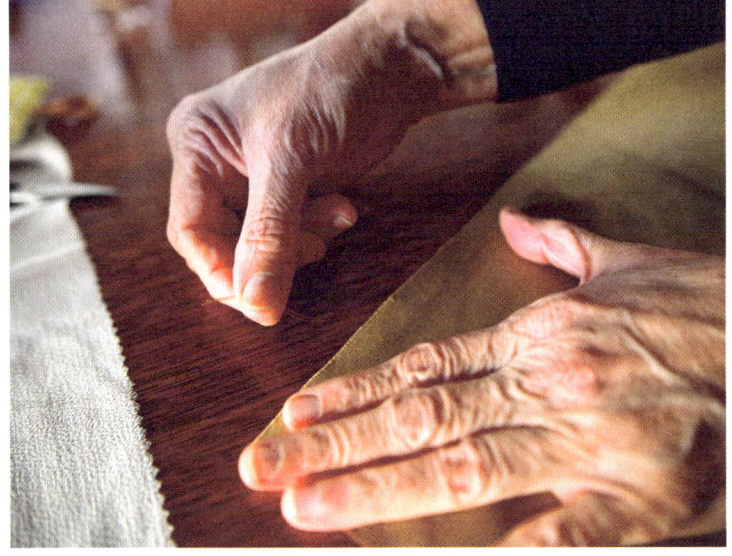

EARTH — HAND

Yen Yen Lo

CLAY BODIES: white and buff raku; terracotta
SURFACE FINISHES: underglaze colours; white and clear gloss glazes; terra sigillata
KILN TYPE: electric
FIRING TEMPERATURE/CONE: 1080–1200°C/1976–2192°F

Yen Yen Lo had a lot of pets when she was growing up in Sarawak, Malaysia, and her Chinese heritage is deeply connected to symbolism through nature, animals and plants. She says she particularly relates to the turtle because it is reclusive and shy, just like her. She has no qualms about spending long hours in her studio and relishes the quiet moments there.

A large part of her working life was spent as a graphic designer in publishing. She grew up with a love of books and wanted to work with typography, paper and design and was successful in this for a long time in Singapore. When she moved to Melbourne, she continued in the same field but the work had become less rewarding, so she decided to leave design work. She had not touched clay since her early teens but took a class at the local community art centre and instantly loved the feel of clay again.

When she tried handbuilding and made her first plate, she heard an actual click in her brain. She knew that this is what she was meant to be doing because it felt so right. The teacher let her find her own way, teaching her just enough to get on with her making but allowing her to explore the medium herself. She still likes to think she has control over the clay, but she knows she doesn't really, that sometimes it doesn't work the way she wants it to. That challenge is part of the fun.

For the first few years, she built in the pinch style but it led to a lot of hand pain. After bringing the pain under control, she began looking for other ways of making that would suit her and found a process of working with slabs and templates. Some pieces start as a cylinder, which is then cut into wedge or leaf shapes (a process called darting) that are then joined, altering the form. Other pieces start out as two identical flat shapes, which are then curved at the edges and joined at the seams to create a whole.

These seams may reflect a memory from her childhood, of a blue claypot in which her mother simmered soups, sometimes for hours, in preparation for dinner. When a crack appeared at the bottom of the pot, her mother repaired it with layers of rice paste. It was a nightly after-dinner ritual to seal the cracks with mashed cooked rice and set the pot on the stove over a gentle flame. 'Whenever I ran my fingers over the bottom of the pot, I could feel the scar from the layers of rice adhesive built up over the years.'

Not only does this process suit her physically by reducing her pain, it suits her work space, which is confined to the table and shelf in her dining room, with the kiln outside in a shed. Her workspace is so small that when she needs to wedge clay, she takes it out to the backyard.

Yen's work starts with a sketch of the 'body'. She might sketch it over and over again, playing with possibilities and decorations before the making. Once the sketch feels right, she templates the design using paper cutouts and keeps refining until the proportions look right. Only then does she cut the pieces and seam them together to create their sculptural shapes. She sometimes burnishes the clay with a spoon to help compact and strengthen it and uses very 'low tech' tools to carve and texture designs into the clay. Her most precious tool is a small wooden spoon her sister gave her, which she can hold comfortably and uses as an extension of her own thumb to help her close the seams. She then uses whatever instrument suits her surface decoration technique to make the mark she wants – a knitting needle to make holes, or the end of a paintbrush.

After that, the pieces 'hibernate' in plastic containers on shelves to prevent them from drying out too quickly. They are marked on the outside so she can easily identify them. She may pull a piece out of hibernation, basing her choice on what mood she is in (snarly teeth probably mean she's been a bit cranky that day!).

Her patterns and decorative elements mostly reference Chinese folk art patterns of flowers and leaves from embroideries, and she looks to Chinese bronzes for shapes. Harking back to her time in book design, she uses a spot glaze in the design that reminds her of a spot varnish that book covers often have.

Yen loves the solitude and creativity of her practice. Seeing her ideas come to life as three-dimensional objects excites her, but she's let down by other people's lack of understanding that this is a career choice. When these thoughts get to her, the creatures can start to show the frustration she feels through their snarling teeth and ridiculously big eyes. These are the feelings that Yen channels into her work. Even though her designs are stylised, simple, inanimate objects, she hopes that viewers can connect with them emotionally.

From her restless mind comes characters of incredible beauty and calmness that are made with great skill. Although it takes time before she's even happy to start the clay work – drawing, redrawing, templating, researching – her work is worth the wait.

Opposite, middle and bottom: Carving and hand forming the sculpture.

Erin Lightfoot

CLAY BODIES: porcelain
SURFACE FINISHES: coloured stains; clear glaze; ceramic decals
KILN TYPE: electric
FIRING TEMPERATURE/CONE: cone 10

Erin Lightfoot has long been interested in patterns and textiles. She has been around ceramics her whole life – her mother, Vivian Lightfoot, is a figurative sculptor. 'I was about four and my mum was studying ceramics. My brother and I would tag along and play outside. I can remember the smell of the outdoor kilns… and being intrigued by their size and structure.'

She studied fashion at Queensland University of Technology, a course she moved from her hometown of Canberra to do. But it wasn't until the two creative forms connected that she thought about ceramics as a medium for her own design work.

In 2011, Erin started to notice prints on ceramics and realised that she could use clay as a canvas for her patterns. This led her to create jewellery, particularly bangles in the beginning. She went back to Canberra and spent six weeks in her mother's studio working on a basic concept and then developing it into a process of production. The process included finding a supplier to get her designs, which she creates using Adobe Illustrator, printed out on underglaze decals specially made for firing to ceramics.

It was a steep learning curve that included having a kiln full of bangles melt, but which ultimately resulted in her first range of ceramic jewellery. Back in her Brisbane studio, she produced work that went into the market and was picked up by bespoke fashion and gift stores, and it wasn't long before one of her bangles appeared on the pages of *Vogue Australia*. The combination of fashion and ceramics, where she could do something unique with her designs, was proving successful.

Erin found the process of slip casting to make the bangles and the use of decals for decorating were the most successful, and this is how most of her pieces are still made. Her first cast vase was based on a chinotto bottle, but she used the decals to arrange the designs one by one, giving each vase its own unique design. This didn't work for wholesale, for two reasons: each piece was taking too long for the price she could charge, and each vase was unique, making ordering difficult for stores. Creating a larger decal that incorporated the full design resolved these issues by creating a limited range of special designs. Decals add another firing to the production process. First comes bisque firing, followed by carving and cleaning. Next comes a glaze firing after being fully dipped, and then the decal is added to the surface and the piece is fired for the final time.

Above: Painting earrings with underglaze.

Above, left to right: Pouring slip into moulds; cleaning back a cast vessel; pouring glaze over the vessel.

Erin received an Australia Council grant that allowed her a four-week residency in Jingdezhen, China, where she worked with highly skilled craftspeople to make the cast moulds for her vessels. She learned how to make a good mould, how to carve and clean the seams, and how to spray glaze. Her time there was pivotal for taking her business forward.

When she returned, her husband, Tang Oudomvilay, joined the business to help develop and produce the slip-cast porcelain range of vessels while she continued to develop the patterns and design new jewellery ranges. Erin's patterns and palette are inspired by modernist and art deco movements, where there is refinement and glamour in recurring patterns.

While the vessels are slip cast, her earring range is all handbuilt and decorated. The range uses porcelain, which is sometimes mixed with stains to create a coloured clay and sometimes painted with underglazes or lustre. Erin has devised a way to cut her earring pieces out by placing the rolled porcelain slab on a plaster slab and putting an acrylic stencil over it. The plaster pulls enough moisture from the clay to stop them from sticking while she cuts out the shapes. The patterns are created by carving in or layering up levels of clay that are joined with slip.

Erin's work is mostly sold through trade fairs and gift markets around Australia. Erin and Tang work towards deadlines for showings and then fill the wholesale orders that follow. 'Ceramics are hard,' Erin says, 'but I also love how you can shape clay into anything, it's an amazing material.' She has an inherent respect for work that takes effort and for the materials used. Fashion, graphic design and ceramics all combine to give Erin a visual language to express her creative voice.

Honor Freeman

CLAY BODIES: superior white porcelain

SURFACE FINISHES: mix of matt glaze from Janet DeBoos and satin glaze from Kirsten Coelho

KILN TYPE: electric

FIRING TEMPERATURE/CONE: 1280°C/2336°F, cone 9

When **Honor Freeman** was a student, she had a part-time job as a cleaner in a motel. She collected the discarded soaps and took them home, knowing that she would need to tell a story with them. They have since become a large part of her work and she has made over 150 moulds of soaps.

Honor wanted to bring greater attention to everyday items and show how you can mark and measure things with them. The slow disappearance of a bar of soap captures the unrecorded passing of time. Using soap as the starting point of her moulds posed some problems. The model has to be waterproof because wet plaster softens the soap, which happened in early trials. To resolve this issue, Honor paints the soap with shellac before making the cast.

Honor uses porcelain slip for her casting. She appreciates both the fragility and strength of the porcelain and the way that the slip changes from liquid to solid. She replicates the various colours by mixing powdered stains into the base clay slip.

After making multiple pieces using the slip-cast method, she works on each piece to make it unique. She carves and shapes the 'bars of soap' while the clay is leather-hard but pliable. She uses various tools, from a butter knife to tiny brushes, to highlight the cracks and marks and shapes that have been captured from the originals. The pieces are then bisque fired in an electric kiln before being finished with a wet and dry sanding process.

Her 2016 installation, *Soap score*, was made up of 656 individual pieces of ceramic soap. These were cast not only from the soap from her cleaning days but from bars that people had sent her, along with their stories. Honor carries the weight of these stories when making the work. Since 2016, she has continued with the soaps and evolved them through different installations, including a series made with gold lustre running through the cracks, referencing *kintsugi*, the traditional Japanese art of ceramic repair using lacquer and gold.

Her electric kiln fits a standard size bucket or besser block – other everyday items that Honor has slip cast. She has also made towels, sink plugs, pillowcases and hot water bottles. She fires fairly regularly because her kiln fills up quickly with these pieces. She is always testing ideas and is rewarded for it when the kiln delivers a happy accident that takes her work in a new direction.

While most of Honor's practice is exhibition work, she keeps up a range of cups, beakers and bowls that she throws and decorates. She likes that people engage with these objects in their lives. But Honor also uses her time at the wheel as a way to switch her brain off and ease her way back into the studio after an exhibition.

Honor starts every day with an early morning ocean swim in Horseshoe Bay on the South Australian coast and most days she feels that she'll do more damage than good if she works past 4 pm. Her family life is important to her; history and stories are important to her. Honor's work is the poetry of her life – it conveys her understanding that some of the simplest objects hold the greatest nostalgia.

Opposite, top left to right: Mixing slip and stain; adding texture to a piece after it has been removed from the mould.

Opposite, middle left to right: Pouring slip into the mould; removing a piece from the mould.

Opposite, bottom right: Detail of Honor's installation *Sillage*, from the exhibition *The Scene is the Seen*, Holy Rollers Studios, SALA Festival 2019.

EARTH — CAST

129

Opposite: *and the tide rises, the tide falls*, 2022, porcelain, stoneware, enamel bathtub, 94 x 152 x 76 cm.

Above: *Fade*, 2021, porcelain, gold lustre, wall installation of 63 objects, 75 x 75 x 3 cm.

Kirsten Perry

CLAY BODIES: mid-fire slip powder; white raku
SURFACE FINISHES: mix of off-white matt glaze, copper oxide, Chun (bluish) and clear glaze
KILN TYPE: electric
FIRING TEMPERATURE/CONE: cone 6

Creative and inquisitive since childhood, **Kirsten Perry** has always wanted to discover how things work and how to make things. She remembers making a clay bird in a tree when she was in primary school. 'I made sure to put on three coats of glaze. A little pot I made won first prize in the local show. We also made our own mudbricks, which were eventually used to build our new art room. We used our feet to mix the clay with straw in metal tanks.'

In secondary school, she leaned towards maths and science, which supported her desire to understand materials. When she left school, she trained as a jeweller and travelled, living in Japan for some time before returning to Australia after a health scare. After this life-changing event, she decided to move away from jewellery and the toxic substances sometimes used in that practice. She wanted to branch out and apply her enquiring brain to another medium, and clay was where she landed.

Ceramics allowed her to create forms that work with shape and colour in new and different ways. Kirsten now works part time in multimedia but spends at least three days a week in her home studio in Melbourne, where she produces her striking slip-cast sculptural pieces – bold and earthy forms that almost seem dug out of the ground.

Using a mid-fire slip, she only has one or two glazes in her range and employs a monochrome collection of mostly white and black clay slips. Creating a limited colour palette has also allowed her distinct forms to become a signature of their own, one that is recognisable in the ceramic and design world. The forms are bold and rough, robust and functional though sculptural, occupying their own space when displayed singularly or as a group.

When Kirsten carves her three-dimensional forms – the first part of the making process – this is where she is most comfortable. It allows her subconscious and creative instincts to emerge. She is addicted to using found and recycled polystyrene, which she cuts into to make the forms she'll go on to cast. The forms reveal themselves quickly, even as she works with patience and care, and the results are immediately satisfying.

Using a hot wire cutter, the shapes she creates have a rough texture that is replicated once when the plaster mould is made, and again when the clay slip is poured in. This texture, the artist's mark, transfers though all three stages: sculpture, mould and final slip-cast piece.

The cutting of the polystyrene gives off toxic fumes but she practices safety and carves outdoors while wearing a mask. Kirsten also uses found and collected cardboard that she folds and shapes to make other forms that, again, she casts with plaster. After casting, the next steps are the pouring and making of the actual pieces. This requires precision timing and patience: as the plaster draws the water away from the slip and it dries, the excess slip is poured out. Once the resulting piece is dry enough to hold its own shape, it is released from the mould. Kirsten has many moulds. She uses some of them over and over, others only a few times. This process allows her to create a limited number of each design, constantly changing and adding new parts and pieces to her collection.

Creating these sculptural forms is a throwback to her industrial design and jewellery training – the three-dimensional form is where she feels most at home. Making larger works from time to time by combining a series of small pieces, Kirsten keeps her work in proportion to her working space. She has many moulds on the go at once, and is always looking for the next design and shape. She is interested in experimenting with other materials, such as concrete, wax and wood, and is exploring how these can be incorporated into her future work.

Previous: A selection of Kirsten's moulds.

Kirsten works year-round on exhibition pieces and commissioned work, and is stocked in galleries throughout the country. Her practice has been a form of therapy. As she works, time passes and she is in a happy place, enabling the healing of traumas, including health issues and family loss. It is her sanctuary – a space that allows her hands and mind to be in a meditative space, a place where she can let her intuition take over.

Below, left and right: Pouring slip into the moulds.

Above, top to bottom: Cast pieces removed from a mould; parts of a mould used to create a sculpture.

FIRE

FLAME

Angus McDiarmid

CLAY BODIES: ironstone; terracotta; locally dug clay
SURFACE FINISHES: own mix of materials
KILN TYPE: woodfired
FIRING TEMPERATURE/CONE: 1360°C/2480°F, cone 12

Nothing about the way **Angus McDiarmid** approaches his work is easy. He digs much of his own clay, uses a kick wheel, and collects wood for his firings. He works eight-hour days through the week and can't understand how people can work at something they don't love. He's totally in love with the clay, the finished form and the lifestyle it grants him.

In 2011, Angus travelled the world for a couple of years, including ten months cycling through South America, where he was invited into locals' homes and experienced living with traditional pottery. He also stayed in India for six months, where he was inspired by the traditional use of terracotta. Studying under an eleventh-generation potter, he lived with his host family, digging his clay and potting, but he didn't fire a thing. It was about learning, not completing finished pieces – recycling the clay each time and starting again. His teacher's father had studied with Shōji Hamada and Bernard Leach, so Angus was learning Indian techniques and the Leach method.

After returning from India, Angus travelled the east coast of Australia, visiting all the woodfire potters he could, making lifelong friendships with many, learning, and sharing a mutual love of the craft. This experience equipped him to build his own kiln and start his pottery career once he established his own studio. He has built his studio and gallery near Lake Weyba in Queensland, where he lives with his wife, Bridget, and their two young children.

Angus digs pure white clay from Lake Weyba's shore, then incorporates about 20 per cent of Keane's Ironstone clay into that body by pugmilling the mixture, creating a clay that is all his own. In using the clay and wood from the area, he understands the sensitive nature of using this local resource. He has consulted with a local Indigenous Elder to learn about the trees – which ones to use, and not use, when cutting wood from his property for the kiln. Honouring the land and the Traditional Owners of the country on which he lives is foremost in his mind as a maker and as a person.

There are many different ways to glaze, or not glaze, vessels for a woodfiring, but Angus chooses to glaze everything that goes into the kiln. He found that raw glazing (where the ash in a woodfired kiln creates the glazes) didn't work well, because the climate where he lives is too dry.

When creating glazes, he learned from his mentor and friend Rowley Drysdale, a local legend in the woodfiring world of the Sunshine Coast potters. Angus considers the size of each work, where it might sit in a home and the use it will be put to. All this informs the glaze, colour and finish of a piece.

Angus fires his kiln three or four times a year, including one firing for a range of terracotta ware. His kiln is fired up to 1360°C/2480°F and can take him up to 38 hours for the entire firing process. This means he always feels like he ends up a little behind schedule in his making routine, but he manages to make up the time and meet the demands of wholesale orders for galleries and stores, and his annual studio sale. He also constantly wants to explore new things, which takes him away from other work.

He is inspired by ceramics and forms from all over the world. His interests include Spanish pottery, which has a lower hip line on its traditional vessels, as well as Mexican and South American wares that are an extension of the cultural styles and colours that can be seen in their architecture and design.

Angus's family and work lives run in parallel on his bush property, which encompasses his home and studio. While he is passionate about his work, he is equally passionate about balancing his time with his family.

His pieces embody a part of himself and he wants those who encounter his work to see not only its beauty but also its substance and the ethics behind it.

Above: Woodfired kiln in use.
Opposite, left to right: Drying shelves; Angus throwing on a kick wheel.

Opposite, top to bottom: Finished collections in Angus's gallery; woodfired moon vase.

Above: Angus's self-built studio.

Kevin Boyd

CLAY BODIES: white stoneware; porcelain
SURFACE FINISHES: metal oxides added to stoneware slip; strontium as a flux and titanium as a glaze modifier – both respond well to coloured clay slips
KILN TYPE: gas
FIRING TEMPERATURE/CONE: cone 9–10

Kevin Boyd is beloved in the ceramics community of Australia for his forty-five-year journey with clay. He is a potter whose career has been balanced between teaching and practice, and both hold his heart in equal measure. He makes his own work when he has time and shares every part of his knowledge with his students – he emphasises the point that he learns much from teaching.

When Kevin first handled clay, he felt it was the perfect medium. He says he didn't seek clay, it found him. From the very first time he sat at the wheel, he could throw a pot – and he felt it was a sign. He also sees this from time to time in some of his students. The love of working with the clay in his hands convinced him this would be his life's pursuit. He set about learning skills to make a career out of ceramics, luckily finding a great community of artists.

Kevin believes that having split his time between teaching and production has allowed his hands, shoulders and arms to sustain a working life well into his seventies. In his career, he has also done slip cast and handbuilding, but he always returns to the wheel.

He works most days of the week in his home studio in Melbourne or teaching locally, and would fire every day if he could. The surprise of opening a kiln is a highlight of his work as a potter, and he enjoys the fact that there is always something going on in the studio – different pieces at different times of their life as a vessel, something always needing his attention.

He chooses to make ceramics that are not just for decorative purposes; he loves that his work has a use. Kevin has always drawn and painted, but those pursuits have always been secondary to clay. When he is working at his best, he gets a spontaneous response to what is forming on the wheel.

For many years, the glaze process has been a major part of his passion as a potter. This aspect of his work is something he is renowned and celebrated for. Kevin often travels Australia, teaching people about glazes and their wonders. He says that glaze is very responsive to clay and, while he is decorating and glazing, if the vessels sends a message to him to say it is right, he listens.

Kevin fires in a gas kiln, particularly enjoying the glaze results a reduction firing can give. He explains that the reduction of oxygen molecules in the glaze and clay gives a piece a finish that can't be achieved in an electric kiln.

He throws with 'the very reliable' stoneware clay and dresses it up with clay slips with the addition of metal oxides. He also loves to use a high-iron-content terracotta to create a slip. His process of producing many test tiles and an almost endless array of combinations of applying slips and glazes is part of creating his distinct work. This trial, error and play with glazing and slips is also why he is so respected and sought after as a teacher.

Kevin is enchanted by the mystery that is clay, and how the volcanic evolution of the earth and the materials we use and reuse to create ware all come from nature. Pottery has taught him much about life – that one must be present when working. His driving philosophy, that the relationship between oneself and the earth is the essence of creation, is embedded in ceramics: born of clay, formed by hands and glazed with a magic blend of materials that melt when fired. Working this way, with materials that surround us all the time, is a way of responding to where we live.

Previous: Decorating using glaze and slip.

Above: Glaze test tiles.

Opposite, top left to right: Preparing and adding sculptural additions to the vessel.

Ray Cavill

CLAY BODIES: porcelain mixed with recycled clays; iron stones; silica pebbles; assorted other textural materials

SURFACE FINISHES: Shino carbon-trap glazes; low- and high-iron glazes; ash glaze; natural ash glaze

KILN TYPE: anagama woodfire

FIRING TEMPERATURE/CONE: cone 13 at the front, cone 11 at the back

Ray Cavill has reached a point in his career when he now only makes work if 'it's got somewhere to go', be it an exhibition or collector. Yet his decades-long career, which has spanned teaching and exhibiting, is in some ways just getting started.

Ray's gallery and studio are in a century-old church he owns in New South Wales. His dream studio includes building an extension to house more studio and teaching space, and an anagama kiln (the name deriving from a Japanese term meaning cave kiln). A kiln on his own land is a promise he made to himself after building many woodfired kilns on other people's properties.

Ray grew up in a house full of interesting ceramics, glass, painting and furniture. After leaving secondary school, he met Martin Kelly, a lecturer and potter who is known for his Shino techniques. Seeing Martin's work in a solo exhibition had a great impact on Ray and led to the career he has forged. He realised he could learn and work in clay for the rest of his life and yet would never know everything. This was the hook, although it would be a few years before ceramics became his full-time career.

His first studio was under a water tank in the country town of Kingaroy, Queensland, where he worked as a primary school teacher. He had studied clay in his teaching degree and when he moved to Kingaroy, he took his wheel and furthered his education with night classes at the local TAFE, where he could use a kiln. At a crossroads, knowing that as a teacher he would have to move to another town, he decided to give up teaching and headed to Newcastle University to study an undergraduate degree in visual art. This is when his real love for clay and form was harnessed and a career path revealed itself. He found great joy in exploring all aspects of his art practice. He did everything he could in as many mediums as he could, majoring in ceramics and minoring in printmaking.

After returning to Brisbane, Ray started teaching at Southbank TAFE. He was there for seventeen years before going it alone and opening Clayschool in an old bakery in Brisbane's West End. Clayschool has been operating for more than ten years and its alumni have acknowledged Ray as having had a big influence in their careers.

During his long career of teaching, Ray has always maintained his own practice. He decided that making his own work was about exploring and discovering the limits of what the clay could do when pushed. Though proficient as a wheel thrower, Ray also forms pieces by hand, literally throwing slabs on a table and pulling them, holding them with his hands and sometimes even ripping them. Then he carves and textures them with tools and his hands, and adds texture with found natural objects that stay the course of the firings and remain embedded in the forms. Working with both the physicality of the clay and instinct, Ray enjoys all parts of the creating process. He sees 'making' the form as only part of the process. Woodfiring, where art, science and complication meet, is also at the heart of his process.

Ray works with many different clay bodies, from fine Limoges porcelain to groggy, earthy clays. Anything 'with a bit of guts', he says. He alters the raw clay, adding ironstone from Stradbroke Island and silica from Broken Head – two of his favourite places. These don't just add to the body of the piece, but the story of it. Sometimes he mixes in terracotta chips or she-oak wood. He is fascinated by how the other materials react, split or melt into the clay. The surprise of the finished result when he opens the kiln is where the goosebumps happen – that is what drives him.

Previous: Compressing the clay with a handmade tool consisting of bamboo and sponge.

Opposite: Wedging clay to remove any air bubbles and pockets.

For Ray, clay is a supremely important material. When placing work in a woodfired kiln, he knows what zone to put the pieces in for the best results, and that the packing and firing techniques are what drive the final results. He says a good potter knows their materials very well, but clay still cannot be taken for granted. The fusion of the clay and the glaze is one of the things he finds most interesting. Ray strives to achieve the best qualities from the clay by the way he forms it and how it comes through the firing. Details of what the fire reveals can been seen and felt within the texture of the piece. Ray continues to humbly chase the magic of the unending parameters of clay, and the feeling of being moved by something beautiful.

Sandra Bowkett

CLAY BODIES: recycled stoneware; local granitic sands
SURFACE FINISHES: celadon; Shino and other stoneware glazes
KILN TYPE: electric, woodfire and reduction
FIRING TEMPERATURE/CONE: 900–1315°C/1652–2399°F

Career potter **Sandra Bowkett** loves the environment where she lives and works, among the gum trees with a pot belly stove in the corner and sunshine streaming through the windows of her studio. Her career has spanned decades and styles, from brightly coloured tableware and decorated fine porcelain vessels to her current passion for earthy woodfired stoneware.

Sandra's home and studio are off the grid. This is where she built her woodfired kiln, which she fires about five times each year. The firings can only happen from late March until November, to avoid bushfire season. She has a second studio space in Tallarook where she does her wheel throwing and uses an electric kiln for bisque firing.

Sandra believes that her work doesn't have anything to 'say' as such – it is more about the simple pleasure of making handmade items to be used. Over the years she has suffered from repetitive strain injuries, so her current practice is thoughtful for her body. She might throw for a couple of days and then have a break. She is usually in the studio by 10 am, after having done work around the home, fed her chickens and perhaps collected wood for the kiln on her wander down to the studio.

Woodfiring is not for the faint-hearted. The wood that is needed for such a big undertaking is collected and chopped from timber on her property. The kiln is stoked for a minimum of fourteen hours, reaching as high as 1315°C/2399°F. Sometimes she fires on her own, at other times with fellow potters. When others are in on the firing, the responsibilities are different and the time is passed with conversations and shared meals. Sandra loves the casual nature of these firings, which have become more community-based. During these firings, she can comfortably impart her more than forty years of experience in a relaxed, casual, mentoring way.

Ash from the fire sits on the pots, revealing which side of the pot faces the flame. Sandra's heavily wooded property is full of black wattle, which has a short life span and is quick to regrow. Helped by her partner, Peter, it is a two-day job to get two trailer loads of timber for a single firing. Preferring to not work with stains, Sandra uses a terracotta liquid slip for minimal decorating on her stoneware forms.

There is another side to Sandra's ceramic heart – her love and dedication to a group of traditional Rajasthani potters in India. She has travelled to India often since her first visit in 1988, when she went to work on an archaeological site. In 2002, a friend put her in contact with a community of village potters, whom she has since visited every two years.

These include her friend Minori and his family, who she has also supported for cultural exchanges in Australia. After a three-month Asialink residency in 2012, Sandra learned to throw off the hump, making chai cups. She was entranced by the fluidity of the work of the potters. She says the Indian potters work in a different way to potters in the West, where she feels we try to control the clay. They know the clay is in control, and let it be. This insight and ethos has led her to retrain her brain and hands, loosening the aesthetic of her forms.

Sandra continues to happily make her pots in the bush. They are simple, beautiful, quietly profound vessels that have found homes all around the country. By organising her life around her firing and work schedule, she has been able to set up an inexpensive lifestyle that can support her practice and life – handmade and perfectly formed.

Above, top: Using a woodfired kiln at night.
Opposite, top: Pieces ready to be fired.

FIRE —— FLAME

159

Sandy Lockwood

CLAY BODIES: own mixes of powdered raw materials
SURFACE FINISHES: white/green stoneware liner glaze; slip outside; salt glaze; ash glaze
KILN TYPE: Bourry-style firebox wood/salt kiln
FIRING TEMPERATURE/CONE: cone 12+

Sandy Lockwood's work is inspired by her surroundings: the colours of the earth, the weathering and ageing of the natural world. She believes that clay has a haptic quality to it – you can sense the touch of the maker and their movement in the finished piece – and that woodfiring can emphasise this.

Sandy took night classes in ceramics in the mid-1970s, and worked at Blackfriars Pottery in Sydney doing glazing and packing and eventually production throwing. She then enrolled in ceramics at the National Art School in Sydney in 1979, and went on to teach ceramics part time at the school from 1992 to 2020. Sandy was awarded a PhD from the University of Wollongong in 2018.

In 1980, she moved to the Southern Highlands in New South Wales, where she lived in a tin shed while she built a woodfired kiln and studio on the property. When the kiln was finished, she started making mudbricks for her house with help from friends. She still lives in the house and has built and modified more kilns over the years. To say she has devoted her life to clay would be an understatement.

Sandy had a deep response to the surface qualities of woodfiring. Not knowing what is going to happen in the kiln is exciting to her, and it is even more exciting when she is working with salt glazing. Today she has three woodfired kilns on the property – two dedicated to salt firings of her own work and a third wood-only kiln that she also uses for workshops.

Sandy makes her own clay bodies using powdered raw materials and adding aged, recycled clay mixed in an old bakery dough mixer. She makes about 200 kilograms of one type of clay at a time and can have up to ten clays on the go at any given time. Sculptural clay bodies are mixed with stones, sand, broken porcelain from discarded pots, and sometimes rocks from ant nests. Developing clay is a constant exploration and she is curious about unknown elements that might emerge from the kiln.

Her work ranges from sculptural to functional, and pieces that combine both elements. When producing a run of functional wares, such as cups, she throws on an electric wheel. When trying new forms, trimming or slipping work, she uses her kick wheel as it gives her more control and a different rhythm. Using both methods also gives her body a rest from being in one position for a long period. Early in her practice, Sandy only ever did raw firings, but for the last twenty years she has bisque fired all her work. She glazes the inside of vessels before the salt firings and all pots are wadded to ensure they don't stick to each other or the shelves.

In the two kilns for salt firings, she does what she calls 'quick firings' at around thirty hours. The larger salt kiln is used for a mix of tableware and sculpture. All three kilns are fired three to four times a year, plus workshop firings. Sandy uses a local timber merchant who delivers plantation-grown wood cut to the right length to fit her kilns. The wood is then split on site as required.

Woodfiring is a demanding job due to having to keep the fire stoked and temperatures on track over a long period. Adding salt glaze into the mix adds another complexity. Sandy buys bags of swimming pool salt to use in the kiln. When the temperature of the kiln is quite high, between cone 8 to 10, she introduces the salt. She lays sheets of bark on top of the wood in the firebox, puts the salt on top and allows the magic to happen. The sodium becomes a vapour and travels through the kiln with the ash, glazing the work by reacting with the silica in the clay, becoming a sodium silicate (glass) glaze.

Above: The process of preparing a woodfired kiln.

In every kiln load, there is surface variety caused by the areas where the vapour reacts – a 'saltier' side and a 'quieter' side. When she is packing the kiln, Sandy considers each piece and how she would like to see the finish. The front of the kiln is more exposed to the flame, so the pots placed there will appear more dramatic due to the heat, ash and salt coverage. Towards the back of the kiln, the appearance of the glaze is more subtle. Some clay bodies also accept the salt more than others. Considerations are made at every stage, but eventually the alchemy is out of her hands. When a result isn't satisfying to Sandy, she will live with it for a while, study and learn from it, and it will then join the shards pile that is used as a fire break.

Even after spending forty years as a potter, there is nothing that Sandy enjoys more than being in the studio, thinking only about the clay that is in front of her, or finding a 'gift from the kiln' in a firing of something unimagined but wonderful. No wonder there is no talk of retiring from this potter.

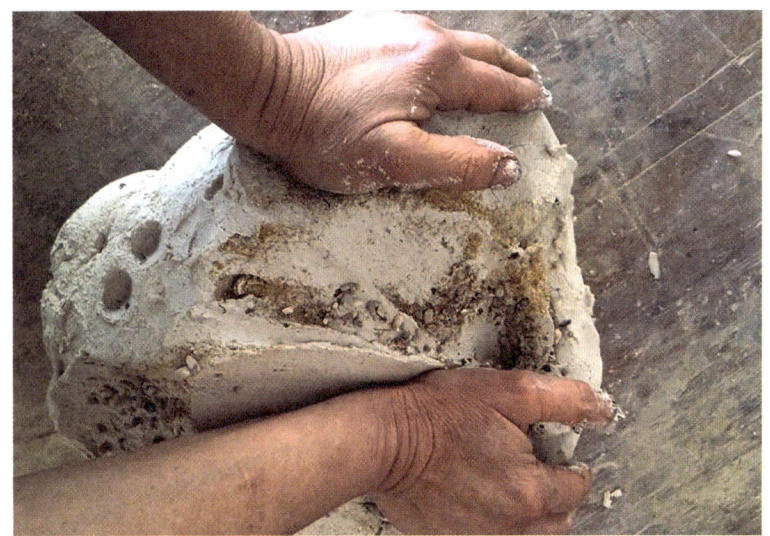

This page, clockwise from top left: Wedging natural matter into clay; unpacking the kiln; works drying in the sun.

Opposite, top to bottom: A sculpture from Sandy's *Unearthed* series; a tea bowl from her *Chawan* series.

164   SANDY LOCKWOOD

Susan Frost

CLAY BODIES: porcelain

SURFACE FINISHES: own mix of glazes from raw materials, using a blend of shiny base glaze and commercial stains for colours

KILN TYPE: electric

FIRING TEMPERATURE/CONE: 1287°C/2349°F, cone 9–10

When you move from a corporate life to an artistic one, it would be easy to change your habits. But **Susan Frost** was happy with the work-week structure of her life and has kept it going even though her studio is at her home. She is driven and focused, and her work requires that level of attention, as it too is seamless and thoughtful.

Her first encounter with ceramics was her parents' fine-rimmed Noritake dinner service – predominantly white, with a delicately sponged leaf decoration, it is simple, elegant and functional. She still has a cup and saucer from this set in her home. On a school excursion to the Art Gallery of South Australia, she was captivated by 'Japanese Girl', a porcelain plate painted by Mortimer Menpes with expressive cobalt brushstrokes. She still looks for it when she visits the gallery.

Susan started taking ceramics in an evening class at the Bristol School of Art when she moved to England with her husband, Andrew, in 2005. On returning to Adelaide, she continued ceramics at Adelaide College of the Arts. After completing her studies, she undertook a two-year associate program at Adelaide's JamFactory. The program allowed her a studio space and full access to the equipment, including wheels, kilns, materials and spray booths. It was here that she met Kirsten Coelho, who became her friend and mentor and for whom Susan now works two days a week. Kirsten has had a profound impact on Susan's practice, and they share a deep interest in glaze outcomes.

Susan works best with a deadline and she is good at focusing her attention. The dream state that precedes the making is also interesting to her. Thinking about a body of work for a show, and the inspiration behind it, drives her to trials and tests to see what is feasible, so she can reduce the possibilities and focus clearly on the outcome. She often completes most of the work in the final six weeks before a show. Of course, that six week period is likely to include seven-day weeks and ten-hour days.

Her real gift lies in colour and design, and her patience in realising those designs in clay and glaze. After spending four months in New York in 2019, where she studied the city's architecture and the collections of its galleries and museums, she created a range of art deco–inspired designs. Starting with completely dry greenware, she draws directly on the wheelthrown vessel, working out not only the one-dimensional pattern but the multiple layers she will create by taping up and sponging back. Finding a tape that would stick and allow her to build up layers while also being easy to remove required much testing. Only once all levels are sponged back does the tape come off and the vessel go in for a bisque fire.

The second design stage is the glaze technique. She uses her hands instead of tongs to prevent leaving a mark. To achieve a continuous smooth glaze without any tool or fingermarks, she does it over two days. On the first day, she glazes the inside, and on the second, the outside. This means that the rim remains unglazed, which she chooses to retain rather than applying additional glaze. Susan has tested and perfected a range of coloured glazes that she mixes with stains, aiming for a tonal match across her work.

Susan loves that small works can have just as great an impact as large pieces. She is interested in making larger works at some stage but recognises that the patterns and dimensions will need to match in order for them to be successful. Like most artists, she struggles with the balance between making objects that challenge her and objects that bring in a more regular income. For a long time, she produced more everyday tableware, which kept her working at the wheel, which she loved. But she missed the expression and research

Above, top to bottom: Sponging back layers of clay to create a design on the vessel; measuring stain to make a glaze that matches the test tile.

Opposite, top: A collection of vessels drying out before being fired.

and testing that comes with exhibition work. To do more exhibition work, she has to find funding in order to keep control of her own practice and give her the freedom to explore what she wants to create.

    Susan loves the immediacy of clay: there are so many possibilities that it is a never-ending quest. When she sits throwing at her wheel, everything else just falls away. Her patience is her superpower, but so is finding so much joy in what she does for a living.

Ulrica Trulsson

CLAY BODIES: stoneware; porcelain
SURFACE FINISHES: mixes own glazes, often containing oxides and stains
KILN TYPE: electric
FIRING TEMPERATURE/CONE: cone 9–10

Ulrica Trulsson grew up in Östersund, in the cold north of Sweden, but, curious by nature, she left to travel when she was seventeen years old. Her curiosity has driven her ceramic practice. Now she calls her studio her haven. Its white walls allow her to focus on the work in front of her without distraction. Her work is captivatingly subtle, sitting somewhere between make-believe and functional, precious and utilitarian.

When Ulrica was in senior school, she did an arts program that gave her the freedom to try many varied art forms, from painting to photography, filmmaking and ceramics. 'I remember sculpting portrait busts in clay and exhibiting them with my friends. We painted ourselves white and sat with our heads sticking out of boxes among the sculptures. In the dimly lit space, it would take visitors a moment to realise not all heads were created equal.'

Later, when she travelled the world, she relied on photography as her creative outlet but she knew it wasn't going to be her medium forever. She settled in Melbourne in 2008 and started classes in ceramics the following year. This led her to a two-year diploma of ceramics at Homesglen TAFE that taught her about clay as a material. Being engaged with the material, seeing the possibilities and testing different processes and methods gave her the core understanding about what she could do, and wanted to do, with the material as an artist.

Ulrica was offered a job at JamFactory in Adelaide. Her time there was instrumental to her working on her artistry in clay. She says wheel throwing felt organic and intuitive to her. 'Centring a ball of clay when you can feel the shift into a form in your hand is exciting.' She speaks of her connection to clay as a collaboration. She connects to the clay in a humble way, knowing when she has to give in to it. She takes time to work through problems, some of which turn out more positively than expected, because this can move her on to 'something more interesting'.

When starting a piece or body of work, she begins with simple silhouettes or shapes. She normally puts in a full work week in her Brisbane studio, but increases her time there in the lead up to an exhibition, while still following the standard cycle of throwing, trimming and drying. Sometimes she faces a double handling, as a lot of her forms are canisters with lids. Ulrica particularly likes these as objects because they are a closed form that you can uncover by removing the lid. She throws them as separate pieces – the body followed by the lid – and combines them in the trimming process. She makes continuous small decisions as she throws a piece, as there are many factors that determine how well the finished pieces sit together. They can melt into each other, or dry or shrink at different rates – every slight movement has an effect on the end result. Her skill in making that look seamless is undeniable.

Ulrica puts the perfectly formed leather-hard vessels back on the wheel and applies a thick slip she has made. Working fast, she uses her hands to create her designs all over. The slip is made from the same clay body as the pot, so it adheres and becomes part of it, but it can also weaken the structure because it becomes wet again. 'I have to commit and work really quickly to avoid any issues.' She uses a heat gun to dry the thick slip layer when she has completed her decoration. She has to carefully monitor the pots as they dry, looking for cracking that she must correct. Finally, she dip glazes to get a consistent and clean finish to the work. In creating these layers of texture, Ulrica still allows a hint of the clay behind. It makes her work intriguing and unique.

Forms and details from the natural landscape are Ulrica's inspiration. She doesn't mimic nature, it flares up her imagination and informs her work subconsciously. Ulrica is a truly humble artist. She gives gratitude not only to all the teachers and fellow artists she has worked with, but to the medium itself. 'Clay gives you gifts, and you're the custodian of those gifts,' she says. It is this belief that gives her the drive to create her unique works.

Opposite, bottom left to right: Using a pottery wheel to paint slip on the vessel; separating the lid from the body to ensure the lid doesn't seal; stacking the vessels into a drying rack.

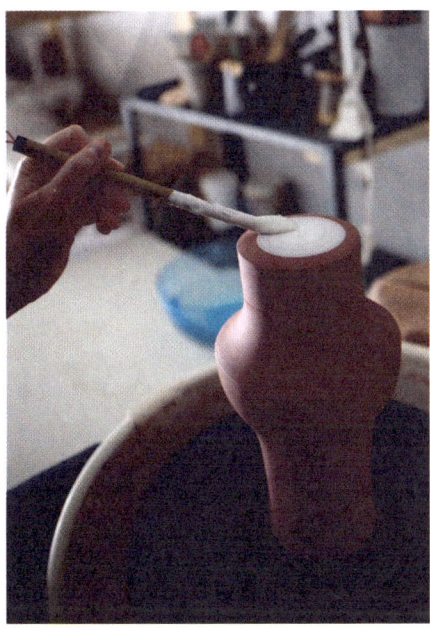

Zak Chalmers

CLAY BODIES: stoneware; porcelain; locally dug clay

SURFACE FINISHES: stoneware reduction glazes; naturally formed glaze from woodfiring

KILN TYPE: woodfire kilns – anagama, catenary arch; gas/soda kiln

FIRING TEMPERATURE/CONE: 1320°C/2408°F, cone 12

Zak Chalmers is the son of a farmer. His earliest memory of clay is making little clay figures at a dam on his family property in South Gippsland, Victoria, where he learned the value of hard work. It is only natural that he has chosen highly physical making and firing techniques in his practice as a woodfiring potter. His teachers encouraged his work ethic and desire to make pottery not just his living but a way of life. After travelling around Australia with his wife, Tania, they settled back where they started, in South Gippsland, establishing a home and studio called Valley Plains Pottery.

Zak is a maker of many things – sheds, buildings, kilns and ceramics – and he loves the mechanics of things. Of his twenty-five-year career as a potter, though overcoming work-related repetitive injuries, he says: this work is his job for life. His property overlooks grass plains leading to the ocean. He and Tania built their family home here, which they share with their three children, and his studio and kilns are only a short walk away.

When talking about his process and work and his love for it, Zak is knowledgeable, calm and happy. It is part of him, not just something he does for a living. He likes that clay is so versatile – that you can make whatever you want and at the end of all the processes it will become stone. His reward is that he gets to do this every day.

Zak's processes have changed over time. He started on a kick wheel out of necessity, as he didn't have power connected to the studio for the first eight years. He had to retire using that wheel due to injury. He now throws his large vases, jugs and a range of tableware on an electric wheel in his solar-powered, off-the-grid studio.

The studio has a gas kiln, which he uses through the summer bushfire season. He fires his two woodfired kilns through the winter months, when bushfire danger is low and the heat from the kiln is warming. He has built all his woodfired kilns himself. His first was an ancient Japanese-style anagama kiln he built in 2001, and the second was a catenary arch kiln he made in 2002. The catenary kiln was pulled down after more than a hundred firings as there was so much glaze built up on the interior that pieces of it fell off and hit the pots. It's been replaced by a new catenary kiln, which he also built, which is fired around six times each firing season.

The anagama is his biggest and favourite kiln, and is fired only once a year. It uses a lot of wood, which he collects all year round. Neighbours on farms in the area let him know when trees have fallen so he can collect the wood. Tania and Zak have also planted more than 400 wattles, some of which have matured enough to be used.

The anagama kiln fits about 200 pots, and to reach full temperature and glaze maturity it is fired and stoked constantly for ninety hours. The results of the firing depend on how the flash of the fire and the flying ash react with the surface of the unglazed pots. Zak doesn't use glaze as a medium, preferring the glaze to form due to the mix of ash and the high temperatures. There is also the unknown of how the ash from different woods gives varying colour and texture. Black wattle gives a deep blue and green, glass-like glaze, for example, while cypress and tea tree appear light green. All this thought and creation forms part of the story of each piece.

Zak throws all his pieces on the wheel and considers each form for its use. Wanting to keep his work timeless, he uses carving techniques to give the work some simple design and lets the alchemy in the firing take care of the rest.

It takes two days to pack the anagama, with the big pots going in first, and the smaller vessels going in last around them. With the act of woodfiring being such a time-consuming but integral part of the life of each work, it could be easy to forget the actual vessel being made. However Zak considers every

Above: Zak's pieces stacked and firing in his anagama kiln.

Above: Finished works that show the ash and fire flash finishes from the anagama kiln.

vessel, its proportion and form. A jug, he says, is one of the hardest to perfect, as it is all about proportion and weight and then considering what happens to that when liquid is added and poured.

The challenge for Zak is to make pieces that will have the long life he intended for them after they are shaped from earth and finished in fire. He is a potter who throws beautiful forms and fires them with such commitment that he achieves timelessness in a seemingly effortless way. It is really anything but effortless, and requires significant amounts of time.

This page: The anagama kiln packed and ready for firing.

FIRE — FLAME

MARK

Amy Leeworthy

CLAY BODIES: stoneware
SURFACE FINISHES: underglaze colours; matt stoneware glaze
KILN TYPE: electric
FIRING TEMPERATURE/CONE: 1280°C/2336°F, cone 9

Amy Leeworthy first made ceramics when she was very young, attending a ceramics class in a local community centre when she was eight or nine years old. She recalls that she was the only person there under the age of sixty. Her teacher introduced her to a range of clay bodies and built her confidence to make large pieces, a feat well beyond her years.

She learned some essential techniques and discovered at that young age that the process of sculpting forms was quite intuitive. She brought her works home and filled her family home with them – dragons, a life-sized head, a bust of a man, bird baths and garden statues.

Amy grew up in Red Hill, Victoria. Early European settlers named the township, which was established on Boon Wurrung Country, for its red clay. She recalls that clay was everpresent when she was growing up – caked onto the soles of her gumboots and slippery on the banks of the dams she swam in. 'I remember making rudimentary vases with my sister – simply balls with flowers stuck in them that would dry and crack in the sun.'

She found out many years later that her late grandmother had been a hobby potter, which gave Amy pause for reflection on her own ceramic pursuits. She can feel the energy in the pots her grandmother made and treasures those pieces she now has in her home.

Many years passed between the community centre lessons and getting into full-time ceramic practice. During that time her interests were still creative, but had shifted to painting, drawing, sculpture, animation and photography. Amy returned to ceramics in 2015 after taking a course at Northcote Pottery in Melbourne, where, after feeling wobbly at first, it all started coming back to her and something clicked. She hasn't looked back since.

During this period of relearning, Amy watched many online videos and went through a lot of trial and error. She also became a mother, and spent any spare moments while her toddlers slept attempting to master the wheel. Bit by bit, she gained confidence in her skills.

Amy lives on the Mornington Peninsula in Victoria, and her studio is in a bungalow behind the house. It is a peaceful place with gum trees and a family of kookaburras keeping watch. She appreciates when her artist friends drop by, as she, like many potters, can find studio life quite isolating. She admits to working quite haphazardly without much structure to her days and weeks, but tries to reserve the mornings for wedging and throwing and the afternoons for trimming and glazing.

Her work schedule is a mix of commissions and pieces for galleries and new work. She enjoys working from home, but with school days for children now making the working hours shorter, she uses night-time hours to load and unload the kiln and even brings some work inside when the kids are asleep.

Amy works with groggy stoneware clays and in a warmer spectrum of colours. She enjoys the texture of the clays, especially any clay that looks like the earth. Her bold forms are left without a shiny glaze as she likes to let the natural texture of the clay come through. She uses matt underglazes for colour, and terra sigillata that she leaves raw or paints over to create a painterly look while still showing the texture. Inspired by textiles and weaving, particularly from artists of the Bauhaus movement, Amy decorates her vessels with bold geometric patterns.

Gaining inspiration from the clay itself, Amy prefers being led by it, intuitively following its mysterious ways. She is interested in the long history of the craft of vessel making and says that 'consciously or not' ancient shapes and forms appear in her work. This connection to the history of making spurs her on. She is honoured that people choose to collect her work and loves that a vase encourages people to bring nature into their homes: from spinning earth to filling a handmade vessel with earth again.

Opposite: A finished vessel by Amy.

Above: Amy wheel throwing a vase in her studio.

David Usher

CLAY BODIES: porcelain; stoneware; white raku
SURFACE FINISHES: underglaze colours
KILN TYPE: electric
FIRING TEMPERATURE/CONE: 1260–1280°C/2300–2336°F, cone 8–10

David Usher is a painter of landscapes, both on canvas and ceramic. Each surface has its own storytelling power, its own visual language, and although the marks and lines may seem to overlap between the mediums, they each have their own strengths. He hopes viewers will be given just enough information within his abstract landscapes to allow them to fill in the rest with their own story in the spaces he leaves. He doesn't want the whole script written.

David first discovered ceramics as a career in the mid-1980s through Kitty Breeden, a Dutch-born studio potter in Brisbane, and his future mother-in-law. He furthered his curiosity and training in his early career with a traineeship with Queensland potter Errol Barnes. Under Errol's guidance, David got to work as a technician for artists William Robinson and Joe Furlonger, learning and being influenced by their practice and skills.

In his early career, David also worked as production potter at Yarra Glen, a commercial pottery in Queensland. Working there refined his throwing skills. In the early 1990s, David was also instrumental in setting up Monte Lupo Arts in Queensland, a studio that provides meaningful work to people living with a disability. He says the purity of the work and collaborations with the artists there was a beautiful time in his life as an artist.

David is working on a doctoral thesis in creative arts and is a ceramics lecturer at the University of Southern Queensland. Teaching is special to him for many reasons, not least because it informs his ceramics practice. It impacts his work, he says, because it reminds him to keep an open mind about what is possible, both from a material point of view and also from a conceptual perspective. He teaches his students that one of the most important starting points is to begin to understand the importance of form and to develop an affinity with the material as a medium for a visual narrative, and to consider how the medium of clay might serve them in creating or telling their story.

In his personal practice, both as a painter and a potter, his mark making is striking and singular storytelling in line and form. A deep love of the Australian bush has been fuelled by years of travelling out west, most notably to a family cattle station north-west of St George in Queensland. This, and other adventures along highways and back roads, have driven his desire to understand the horizon line, the shapes and shadows of the land, trees, creek beds and sky, and the spaces between. He talks of how road tripping and watching the land 'spin by' is much like the lines and marks he spins around the vessels he throws. He also spends time motionless, 'en plein air', observing the landscape, curious about the way the earth and shadows, trees, light, and clouds all work together. Then he picks it apart in an abstract reaction to these views, making his own interpretation and visual language.

Though never wanting to choose between his mediums, David believes that using clay offers a closer link to the imagery he depicts because he is literally painting the landscapes on earth and making the form his paintings live on with his hands.

He finds throwing meditative. When he needs to calm anxiety, he turns to the wheel not the paintbrush. He appreciates that ceramics is a medium where you can make something from a lump of clay. The form's surface is a response to these moments and although he may have prepared a specific weight for a number of pieces, he never really knows what forms he's going to run with when he sits down at the wheel, other than that he is throwing a vase or a bowl or a plate.

He is always mindful of how the landscape will sit on the surface, but that too is often a response to the nuances of each form once it has been created. He has used a shiny clear glaze on much of his ceramics through the years, but some of his more recent works leave the outside devoid of glaze. The stone-like

Above, top to bottom: Wedging clay; painting with underglaze on a wheelthrown vessel; a finished landscape vase.

rawness of the clay under the surface paintings made using underglazes and oxides creates a landscape painting seemingly on a rock formation or raw earth.

Despite his long career as a potter and exhibiting artist, David feels he is only getting started. He says his ceramics are really like 'stretching a canvas, but with clay'. He appreciates the function of pottery, that you can 'eat off a painting', and that in a world that can be precious and elitist about art, there is a playfulness in being irreverent about the function of a piece of tableware. That you 'can stick a bunch of flowers in a painting' says it all.

Irene Grishin-Selzer

CLAY BODIES: white earthenware; clay dug from Waywurru Country (Ovens Valley, Victoria)
SURFACE FINISHES: underglaze colours
KILN TYPE: electric
FIRING TEMPERATURE/CONE: 1145–1180°C/2093–2156°F

Irene Grishin-Selzer's practice works in two distinct parts: her ceramics design company, Iggy & Lou, and her art practice. She likes the rhythm and process of making to order, but also allows time to develop new products, to research, reflect and experiment. There aren't many days that are alike for Irene – good scheduling is the key, as is her creative energy.

Her Melbourne-based design business was started in 2003 and focuses on homewares, vases, candleholders and jewellery. Primarily the work is slip cast in moulds that Irene has designed or collected. The slip for these pieces requires perfect consistency so that they come out of the moulds cleanly. The vessels are reminiscent of ancient forms, large voluminous vases and pitchers with finishes that make them appear to be from a long-past age or found at the bottom of the ocean. Clean as they are when they come out of the moulds, once they are leather-hard Irene creates their unique qualities by 'slopping on' thick slip and other clay scraps mixed with anything natural that will burn off in the kiln, leaving layers of textures and deliberate surface crazing. She stresses the importance of her vessels being well glazed inside and getting to the right vitrification, so they are watertight and functional. She then feels more free to experiment with the outside of the forms.

Her work schedule runs at the pace of the wholesale and online orders. Her pieces are popular with interior designers, stylists and magazine editors, and find many homes. Irene works ahead with some of the more popular forms and has them bisque fired and ready to colour glaze to fulfil orders more readily. With drying times differing depending on the time of year, these steps all make a difference.

It is important for Irene to give time to her art practice: clay paintings and abstract sculptures. When in her second studio, in the Ovens Valley, Victoria, she digs dirt and clay and sand loam from the ground and mixes it with porcelain slip and other pigments to paint onto clay tablets. These are mostly abstract landscapes and she often doesn't know exactly how the work will come out until the clay is fired and the organic material is burned away.

Her clay paintings are a deep part of her practice, and her framed works are exhibited in galleries around the country. Irene sees these works as a form of abstract cartography. When building up the layers to form textures and marks, these pieces, although paper-thin, have the strength of stone when fired.

This idea of the enduring quality and strength of clay came to her early. At the age of nine, she saw an exhibition of the Chinese Terracotta Army. 'I was mystified at how old the pieces were and that they'd been buried underground for so long. After the show we walked around the gallery looking at paintings and drawings and I remember realising they wouldn't be able to survive being buried under dirt for all those years. It was the first time I thought of clay as this kind of wonderful, ancient and magical thing.'

Connection to the sea, the land and the earth are all present in Irene's work. She is keen to experiment with mixing elements and leaves the outcome to the alchemy of the kiln. She has a small kiln that she uses for her experiments, because she can see results quickly and either continue or return to the drawing board. Her favourite thing and her biggest challenge is the surprise she gets from the kiln.

Having worked with clay for thirty years, Irene still feels she hasn't done half of what she wants to with this medium. 'The possibilities are endless.'

Opposite, top right: Marking on clay tiles to create clay paintings.

Opposite, bottom left: Irene adding textures to the slip cast piece.

Katherine Wheeler

CLAY BODIES: porcelain; white stoneware
SURFACE FINISHES: underglaze colours; colouring and marbling stains into clay body; gold and silver lustre
KILN TYPE: electric
FIRING TEMPERATURE/CONE: cone 10

Katherine Wheeler spends as much time working inside her house by the fire and television as she does in her studio. She lives in a cold climate, so it's much warmer inside the house, and she is also a night owl who is very proficient at moulding earrings and rings while sitting comfortably in her lounge in the evening with her family and pets.

Katherine studied fine arts in silver and goldsmithing at RMIT in Melbourne but was always inspired by her father's ceramic skills. 'My siblings and I would spend a lot of time making entire farms out of clay. We'd be so excited when he opened the warm kiln and we fished out our small, fired creations from between his pots.'

In 2008 she did her first collaboration of jewellery with a ceramicist. From that experience, she knew clay was going to take priority as her creative material of choice.

Katherine shapes clay quite organically, choosing mostly to handbuild and mould her creations. She is particularly well known for her sculptural coral rings, which are made with porcelain and textured or painted with ceramic underglazes. Her work speaks to her love of the beach and the shapes of nature to be found there.

Inspired by days at the beach and wanting that feeling to be kept alive through something wearable, Kate paints 'creatures' that are based on the patterns and textures she sees on the shoreline. The combinations of earthbound items mixed with sea treasures – like feathers that are found tangled in seaweed – make her think about how they have formed these one-off patterns. This imagination and imagery is unique to Kate and her mind. It is her design language and it is hard to imagine someone else having the same style.

While the concept of the designs sounds otherworldly and potentially hard to connect with, her use of those designs in everyday pieces of jewellery or small plates and cups makes them easily appreciated and much loved. She often creates her own porcelain clay colours by wedging coloured stain to achieve a new coloured clay. Sometimes she marbles stain colours together with the white porcelain clay to create completely unique clays.

This brings another level of complexity to the work, which is then often finished with her painting patterns using underglaze colours and clear glazing over the top. She likes the idea that her work might be considered quirky but, make no mistake, wearing Katherine's jewellery is wearing a piece of art. Katherine has so little desire to duplicate her work that she deliberately doesn't document her mixes of colours, ensuring that the next time she makes a similar work, the output will always be unique.

Within her studio, she has room enough to make jewellery, small pots, wall pieces and small sculptures. The size of her work relates in some ways to the size of her workspace. Drying items need to leave room for others to be decorated or fired. Her process is more organic than planned, which suits her well. As most of her work is sold through design markets or her online store, there is no expectation about what pieces she needs to make. Even her wholesalers are happy to order in general terms of 'earrings' or 'cups' and sell what she has available at the time.

Katherine is never short of new ideas or new processes. She has always admired her potter father's willingness to give anything a go. Her biggest challenge is finding the time. She definitely wants to keep learning from her father and is interested in making glazes with him.

Above, bottom: Painting fine lines on a porcelain ring with underglaze.

In the meantime, she also surrounds herself with collected objects, including her son Max's 'ghost' sculptures that are a few years old now. She loves their personalities and they are a constant reminder of the time he spent in the studio with her.

For her collectors, it is how they have interpreted her designs and how they feel when wearing them or using them. This is why people connect to her work.

Laura Pascoe

CLAY BODIES: porcelain; white stoneware; buff raku; recycled mixes
SURFACE FINISHES: mixes own stoneware glazes using cobalt, copper, iron, titanium and magnesium oxides
KILN TYPE: electric
FIRING TEMPERATURE/CONE: 1280°C/2336°F, cone 10

Laura Pascoe worked as an architect for a number of years and while she will always look at her work through the lens of an architect, she is also an artist, a mentor, a gardener and an environmentalist. Clay allows her to escape the rules of architecture. She mixes and recycles clays, experiments with glazes and isn't too careful with measurements – and sometimes suffers cracks because of it – but she would rather push the boundaries of the clay than live within the constraints of it.

Her energy is intoxicating. She is a partner in a human-centred design consultancy, Surroundings. She is a director of Vacant Assembly, a gallery, pop-up store and flexible studio spaces for artists in West End, Brisbane. Somehow, she also finds time to spend at least two days a week in her own studio at Vacant Assembly, among the endless stream of artists hiring the spaces.

To understand Laura's work is to understand her connection to form and nature, two things she takes very seriously. Her work with Suzie Wiley, her partner in Surroundings, highlights the same combination. They develop tools that help people understand what they need in their homes and how to prioritise decisions. It was when testing one of their own decision-making tools that both women assigned learning pottery as a long-term goal. Instead of waiting until they were older, they signed up for classes at Brisbane's Clayschool in 2013.

Laura feels very centred and focused when she is wheel throwing. It is a process that, if not given undivided focus, can quickly go off course. She loves the contrast of making work with fine rims and heavy bases.

But it's the next two stages that allow her the most freedom in her work. Once her work is thrown and almost dry, she uses a variety of tools to shape and mark it. The decision about where to make the first mark is spontaneous, and each subsequent mark is made intuitively as she swaps from one tool to another. Informed by landscapes and nature, she creates abstract valleys, mountain ranges and forests using tools made mostly from metal or bamboo. She mixes stains and oxides with underglaze to create the colour, and her brushwork is intuitive and responsive to each piece. As the glaze falls into the carved impressions, the stain highlights the textures. The glaze has the opportunity to pool and thicken, giving it a darker appearance; as the glaze thins out, it appears lighter and more luminous.

Laura's studio has been partly stocked with materials from retired Brisbane potter, Pam Cox, who put her whole studio of materials up for sale. It would have been difficult to find a more considerate buyer than Laura, who documented everything she purchased. Laura has coveted glaze materials from the 1970s, particularly the copper oxides, and adores seeing Pam's writing on different tools and vessels in her studio. Pam's tools, combined with those that Laura brought back from China when she did a ceramic residency in 2018, provide her with a wide range of tools from which to choose. As part of her residency, she created her own slip casts for pendant lights that she makes using porcelain and her same marking and glazing techniques.

Before Vacant Assembly, she had her studio at Mappins, a nursery in West End. It was there that she learned how to make the right kind of planters for specific plants. Her exceptional range of jewellery, cups, bowls, vases, pendant lights and planters is a great example of Laura's commitment to making functional pieces that are also beautiful and unique.

Previous: Painting details using oxide and stain.

Opposite, middle: Laura's recipe mix for black stain.

Mel Robson

CLAY BODIES: porcelain; black, yellow and warm stoneware; red terracotta

SURFACE FINISHES: a recipe for a cream matt glaze, a matt black glaze recipe from Kevin White, or no glaze at all

KILN TYPE: electric and gas

FIRING TEMPERATURE/CONE: cone 9

Mel Robson has always been a working artist. Her work is a mixture of functional pottery and installation work, and all of it tells a story. Her obsessions change but advocacy is always at the heart of what she does Her work tells stories of the past and present and her functional wares have a strong narrative, often portrayed through a minimal design that defines her style.

She first studied ceramics at Southbank Institute of TAFE in Brisbane, followed by an undergraduate degree at Southern Cross University, and then a mentorship program through the Australia Council with Canberra-based ceramic artist Patsy Hely. Now the coordinator of the art department at Charles Darwin University in Alice Springs, she jokes that sometimes she thinks she learns more than her students; such are the never-ending lessons of ceramics.

Mel moved to Alice Springs in 2010 and this has had quite an impact on her work. When she isn't working at the university, she fits in at least two days a week on her own practice. The balance of her time is taken up teaching and engaging with the community through arts projects.

In 2019, Mel worked on an installation piece, *Mind the Gaps*, with the Women's Museum of Australia. Mel researched ceramic objects and images from the museum's collection and transferred them onto ceramic tiles she made to fit the cracks in the museum's walls and pathways. She used decals to transfer the images onto the tiles and, once fired, she embedded the pieces throughout the museum. Her aim was to create a reminder of stories that are often forgotten or overlooked in the noise; the ceramic pieces became visible reminders of the past.

Mel has a strong moral compass when it comes to using the medium of clay and the message it can send. A recurring theme in her work is that of using maps as a design on her vessels. When she moved to Alice Springs, her mapping series was a way for her to get to know the place. They tell the story of a place, and when researched properly, they can expose the problematic history of dispossession. The very act of creating a map creates division and boundaries, and inevitably becomes political. We all use them – they give us an idea of our place and identity and show us where we come from. Looking deeper at the words used on maps reveals how emotive they can be, which is why Mel uses them in her work.

One of Mel's other concerns is the use of clay and its environmental impact; once clay is fired, it lasts forever. There are vast numbers of pieces fired during her classes that aren't worthy of an unending life, so Mel's students don't fire their works until the final weeks, and even then, they can only choose a couple of pieces. What isn't fired is broken up, recycled and reused. Not only does that practice work within Mel's classroom and philosophy, it gives the students a basis for their future making, so they only fire what is good.

She practices what she preaches. When she inherited her grandmother's collection of fine pink and gold porcelain teacups, she deliberately broke them to use in her work. 'She would have been horrified!'

In her personal practice, she made a conscious decision to only make small-scale pieces. Her mark-making tools range from ice-cream sticks and needles to nails pushed into a cork. She practices the philosophy that no matter what you push into or drag along clay, it creates a mark. It doesn't have to be an expensive tool.

The use of decals on her porcelain pieces gives her the opportunity to use original handwriting from letters or sewing patterns from women in her family. Her time in Alice Springs has also inspired abstract painted landscapes

Above, top and middle: Adding decals to wheelthrown cups.

Opposite, top: A clay bed in the Northern Territory, Australia.

on her work. She sees the beauty of the landscape, rock formations and the light – 'it isn't lost on me'. Her minimalist approach to mark making is to pair it back to find the pure essence of what she is trying to convey, finding it is often the simplest way to get a feeling, idea or sense of place across to the viewer.

Mel always has work in progress, but she doesn't like to commit to making too much of any one thing because clay offers endless opportunities and she likes to move on. About clay, she says, 'There's always something to learn from, and once you have a small glimpse of what it can be, you just want to keep going'.

Naoko Rodgers

CLAY BODIES: white and dark stoneware; white raku
SURFACE FINISHES: underglaze colours; mixes own glazes with stains and oxides
KILN TYPE: electric
FIRING TEMPERATURE/CONE: oxidation firing to cone 9

Naoko Rodgers is also known by her distinctive business name: 'dots and lines 10 to 1000'. In Japanese script, the character for 10 also means 'dots' and the character for 1000 also means 'lines'. In translation, the name is Naoko's way of joining her Japanese heritage with her Australian life.

The name also alludes to the patterns that are a significant element of her design. Her style is undeniably hers, even with such seemingly simple marks. Naoko works with her hands instead of the wheel, building most of her work from slabs using pinch and coil methods. Using her hands this way, she feels more freedom in how she creates and more connected to the clay.

Naoko was born and raised in Tokyo, Japan, and moved to Queensland in 1995. She had always been creative but had never used clay as a medium. In 2013 she took a class at the Gold Coast Potters Association and instantly knew clay was for her. Working mostly in high-fired stoneware, Naoko creates work that is both functional and well designed. She wants her work to be interesting from any angle, to give the beholder different points of view depending on how it is held or seen – in their hand like a cup, spun around on a table, or on a shelf if it is a vase.

Naoko works in her home studio in Queensland's hinterland. Here she does all her making, testing and firing. She finds her time in the studio very calming; it is her time, when she isn't needed by anyone and can focus her whole mind on the work. She works most weekdays and is constantly inspired by the love for her work that her collectors share with her. Working with clay is a deeply personal thing for her – her energy goes into each piece and out into the world. Naoko's work has been shown in galleries around Australia and Japan and she also sells it online.

Her work is recognisable in the best way. Functional pieces with character are driven by her way of decorating and choice of clay and glazes. Her forms are not always traditional – vases with long necks and large bases and cups with extra-wide handles – yet they always have a sense of balance. She is inspired by the forms and patterns in African woven baskets and lidded cooking vessels, and this design element is often translated in a small way into her pieces.

Naoko's choice of clays and finishes is often unexpected – groggy, dark stoneware that she carves into and white raku with smooth matt glazes. She uses many techniques, including sgraffito and wax resist, and draws with underglaze pencils and crayons on bisque ware. She is particularly well known for her black outline work, which she uses on pieces that suit outline decoration, creating almost cartoon-like drawings. Using a black underglaze pencil, she draws the lines on the vessel after it has been bisque fired. In testing, she found that a standard clear glaze was smudging the lines, but she resolved the issue by using a matt glaze instead. The flatness of the matt finish, along with the drawing that is layered under it, gives her work a unique look.

She draws her ideas before attempting to apply them to her pots. The ideas sometimes keep her up at night and she needs to write or draw them down immediately. This excites her and she looks forward to the next day when she can get in the studio and try out the ideas.

Naoko is conscious that each piece she makes is individual, not a multiple of the same, preferring each to have its own character in shape and design. She is also grateful for mistakes, knowing that ceramics is about timing, such as when she has missed the time to add pieces to work that has dried too far or the weather has impeded the execution of an idea. She honours every piece of work, perfect or not, as offering a learning moment. It is often mistakes that have led to some of her favourite pieces.

Opposite: Handbuilding cups using the pinching method.

Working with clay gives Naoko great joy. She is particularly interested in why something doesn't work out as expected but understands that the clay belongs to Mother Nature and she will have her say. Naoko's ongoing learning experience with clay means she will never get bored and will be making for a long time yet. As she says, 'Pottery has sure become my lifelong partner.'

Niharika Hukku

CLAY BODIES: porcelain
SURFACE FINISHES: underglaze colours; transparent glaze
KILN TYPE: electric
FIRING TEMPERATURE/CONE: 1180°C/2156°F

Niharika Hukku works every day. Not all day, but every day. She doesn't have a favourite part of the ceramic making process – to her they are all enjoyable, but each is different enough for her to know when it is the right time to work on what. For her, throwing pots is like meditation; it gives her a quiet mind.

She often opens the garage door, which backs onto a laneway behind her converted warehouse in Sydney. She enjoys the space and chats with neighbours as she expertly throws each pot. When she really wants to challenge herself, she pulls in the neck of a vessel to see how small a hole she can get at the top.

When she is throwing her pieces, she rarely considers the form in relation to the hyperreal painting that will later decorate the vessel. She may have a painting in mind if the pot is a bowl with painted fish swimming around it, or a streetlight post that would require a taller, straighter vessel. Her choice of subjects for her paintings comes from everyday life, from observations of street life in the city to the vast skies of Australia. When she arrived from India via Indonesia, Singapore and New Zealand, she felt overwhelmed by how much nature was around her, even in the city – the different types of birds, the blue of the sky and the white of the clouds against it. Her hyperreal painting is her way of trying to capture those moments.

Despite her painting style, she is not a perfectionist, choosing instead to consciously stop at a point before it becomes perfect. She adds something that just takes it away from perfection – a speck of white in the eye of a bird or a light flash on the scale of a fish; those details are fun to do.

There is nothing easy about this kind of painting onto ceramics. There are more limitations when working with the underglaze than when using oil paints to achieve the same results on canvas.

She uses a mid-fire porcelain which, once it's bisque fired, she sands and washes until it is smooth. She only paints underglazes on the outside of her vessels, purposely leaving them with a slightly tactile and more natural feel than if an overall glaze was applied. Only the inside of the vessels is fully glazed.

Niharika is often asked how she achieves the incredible realism in her paintings. Her answer is simple: years and years of practice. Her collection of brushes is huge, ranging from $2 shop brushes to very expensive specialist ones. She says tools become a part of your hand, so you have to keep trying different ones until you find the ones that suit your own way of painting.

When she moved with her husband, Ronojoy Ghosh, from India to Indonesia, they both worked in the creative departments of advertising agencies. It was here that she first started learning pottery. They then moved to Singapore, where she found a ceramics studio where her teacher would let her stay on after the rest of the class finished. From here, they moved to New Zealand where she began to sell her work. Next came Sydney, where she finally started a full-time artist's life. Ronojoy still works in advertising and they are both children's book illustrators.

Niharika's creative work doesn't always come easily. There are days when it doesn't work out, hours spent painting a vessel only to have it fail in the firing. When it does work, it is incredibly rewarding because it comes from her heart.

Above: Wedging and throwing the clay.

Above: Painting details onto the vessels using underglazes.

Penny Evans

CLAY BODIES: white and black earthenware; stoneware

SURFACE FINISHES: underglaze colours; red iron oxide; pooling glazes; misfire glazes; clear and coloured glazes; mixed media

KILN TYPE: electric

FIRING TEMPERATURE/CONE: 1100–1300°C/2012–2372°F

For **Penny Evans**, truth telling is most important and her art practice has always focused on ways to better understand herself, where she comes from and who she is. She has healed herself through her work with clay and her understanding of her Indigenous identity, but in the process, she has had to confront many lies and denial. This knowledge gathering has made a huge difference to her art practice and her identity.

Penny was born to a mother of Kamilaroi descent and a white father but she didn't start to connect with her Aboriginal cultural heritage until she was in her late teenage years and studying ceramics. During the 1988 Bicentennial celebrations, a huge demonstration protesting the dispossession of Aboriginal peoples was a pivotal moment in Penny's life that helped her understand her family history and the broader Australian story of colonisation.

When Penny finished studying at the Sydney College of the Arts, she worked at Chowk Ceramics in Sydney where she had a studio and a residence. Over eight years she produced a large amount of functional pieces with her signature graphic design sgraffito work. This included a commission through Gavala Aboriginal Art Centre for the Kamilaroi ceramics collection for Sydney's 2000 Olympics.

Penny says she 'lived an uncomfortable life', using drugs to help her manage the generational trauma from government policies that negatively impacted Aboriginal families, hers included, throughout the 20th century. She spent a year in The Buttery (a residential drug and alcohol rehabilitation centre near Byron Bay) as a result of this trauma. She didn't move back to Sydney, instead moving to Lismore in 2003.

Penny has built on her early prolific years of making functional wares and moved into more conceptual work that speaks to her identity. Her studio is on her property and she works and produces daily. Clay is her main medium and she incorporates mixed media, including natural materials and objects from her time spent on Country. She has two kilns – one test kiln and one larger one that she also rents out to other local potters in need of firing.

Clay allows her more possibilities than other mediums. She loves playing with clay, 'manipulating it and squeezing it in shape'. She incorporates the practice of carving – a large part of her Kamilaroi heritage – into her clay practice. One of her favourite stages of work is when the clay is leather-hard and ready for her to carve into.

Penny has also done larger-scale installation works, such as *Language of the Wounded*, where she uses clay to represent artefacts and talks of the horrific drought of her ancestors' Country during the 2010s. For other works, she has collected kitsch Aboriginal objects and makes moulds from them. In her work *Trophy Wife*, the face of a woman has been made this way and she has used earthenware and underglazes of blue, black and yellow to represent bruises from frontier violence and domestic violence inflicted on Black women. Echidna quills, which she collected from roadkill, give protection to the spirit of this piece.

Regional living allows Penny easy access to Country, where she spends a lot of time. She takes out a bag of clay and teaches in her cultural way, of watching and working and talking. At the same time she is teaching people how to make a clay goanna, she is listening to stories being told to her around the circle and understanding the symbolism more deeply. As she says, 'The more we understand the symbols, the more we understand the stories. There is so much power and magic in stories, even if they are hard to tell.'

Above: *Trophy Wife* by Penny Evans. Underglazes and glazes used with sgraffito techniques have been used to create the artwork.

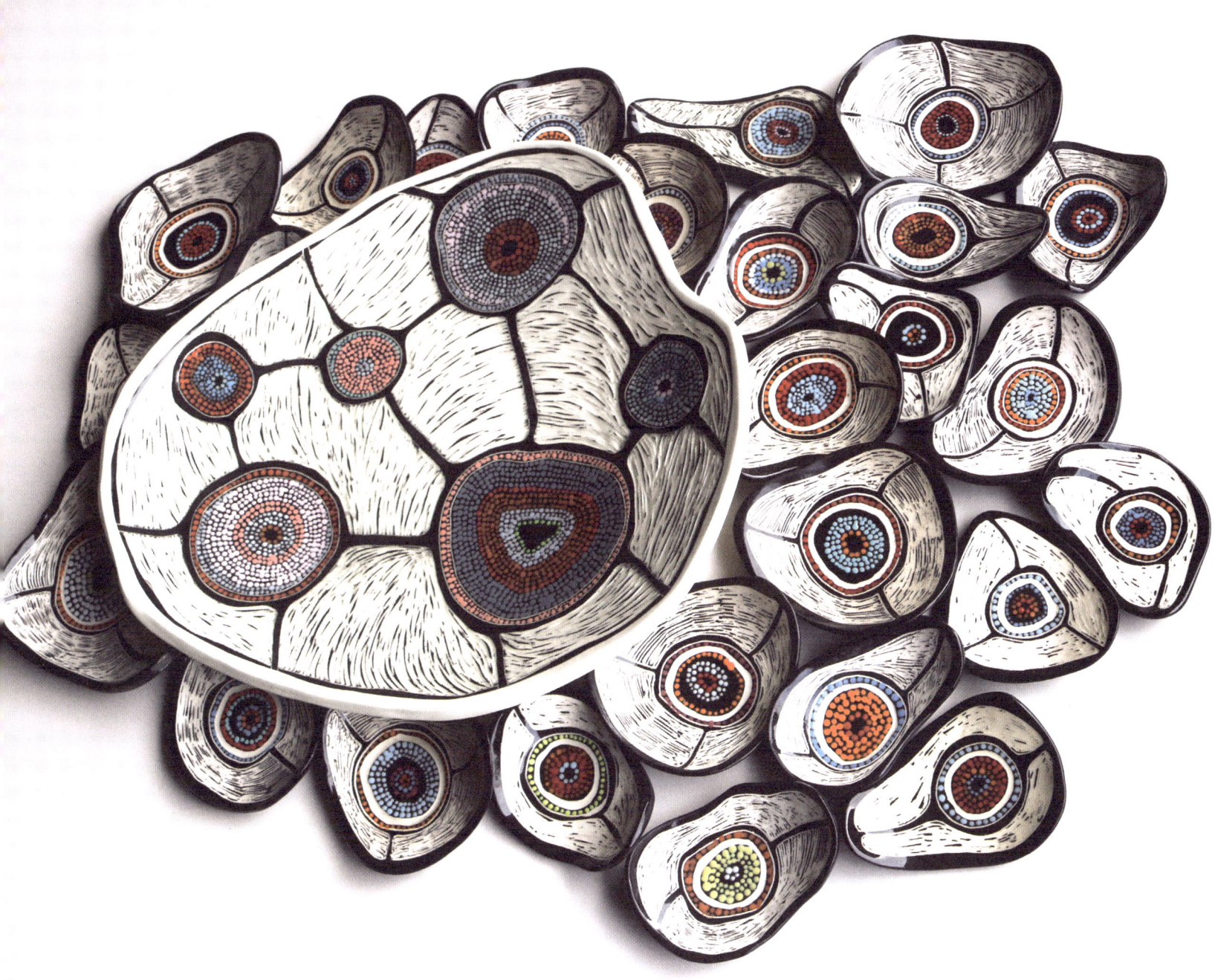

Above: *Meeting Places* by Penny Evans.

Penny is equally passionate about the making as she is about the message and has committed fully to clay as her medium. She moves between the repetitive practice of functional ware to more sculptural work, where different making process, from the 'humble' coil to wheel throwing or pinching and manipulating by hand, are all options for her. Her studio time and her hands in clay are her calm space, a place of meditation. If she can make the time to honour that, she believes her best work is yet to come.

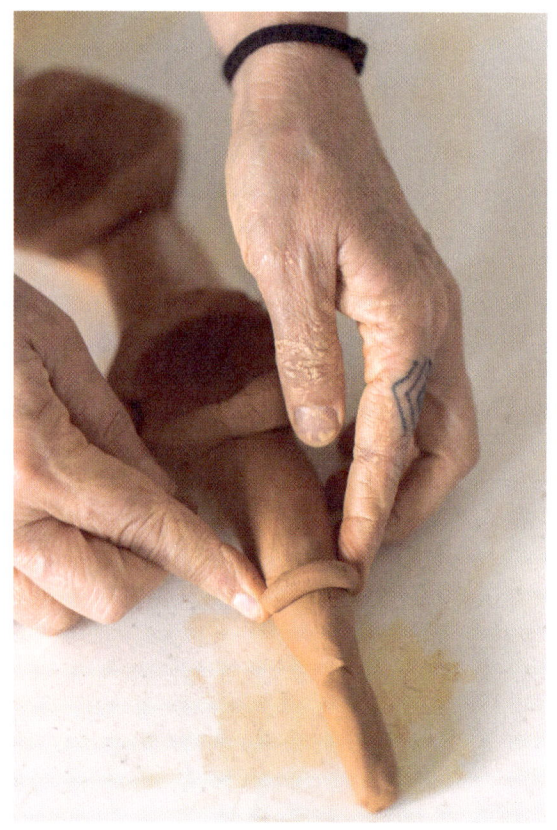

Opposite: Hand forming sculptures.
Above: Penny working in her studio while surrounded by finished works.

Pru Morrison

CLAY BODIES: porcelain; powdered porcelain; stoneware; earthenware
SURFACE FINISHES: clear glaze; clay body stains; terra sigillata
KILN TYPE: electric
FIRING TEMPERATURE/CONE: earthenware 1100°C/2012°F; stoneware and porcelain 1240°C/2264°F

Pru Morrison grew up in in a household that encouraged the discussion of politics and social injustices. She still has a lot to say but she uses her ceramic work as a platform for her thoughts and opinions. Some stories are sad, others are confronting, but they often hold a lot of humour.

Pru studied visual art at the City Art Institute in Sydney then started work as a photographer. She didn't find it rewarding, so she moved to printmaking instead. In this male-dominated industry, she was the only woman in her team and was only paid 72 cents per hour compared to her male coworkers' $1. When she took her employer to task, they admitted it was because she was a woman and said she wouldn't be paid any more. So she quit. The number 72 can be found throughout her work – she is rightfully still angry but she channels it into her work.

After quitting, she travelled the world for a decade. She worked in New South Wales in the snow season and followed the snow around the world. Her artistic outlet was designing T-shirts as gifts for friends, and she made a name for herself on the ski circuit. After ten years, she returned to her home town of Dubbo, in New South Wales. Just outside the town was a pottery – Yarrabah Pottery – which made tableware for the town. The owner said she could have a job if she learned to throw. Pru moved to Brisbane to do an advanced diploma in ceramics, but during the two years she was studying, Yarrabah Pottery closed down.

Pru stayed on in Brisbane. The course made her feel her art had returned to her through ceramics, and she saw how she could use it as a platform for her voice, not just with words but with sculpture and functional wares. During this time, she also connected art with functionality, a unique trait of using clay as a medium.

In her home studio in Queensland, Pru starts by drawing out her ideas. Sometimes it starts with a sketch of the form, sometimes drawings that will merge with a form later. With no lack of content for her satirical illustrations, Pru writes down all her ideas, although she knows she won't realise all of them in her pieces. She seeks out vintage kitchen items that she can use to mould clay around, giving her work layers of meaning.

There is a unique look and feel to Pru's ceramic pieces, thanks to a process she has spent time developing. She makes her own terra sigillata slip, a mix of demineralised water, Dispex and a powdered colour stain. Before painting it on, she sketches out the design in pencil directly onto the piece, then 'colours it in' by painting a couple of layers of the different colours of terra sigillata onto the piece and immediately scratching into the surface. Pru designs with tunnel vision, she says, and often doesn't know when to stop. However, she hasn't regretted anything she's added to a piece'. She averages fortnightly firings and always glazes the inside of a vessel to ensure it is functional, but adds spot glaze to the designs on the outside when it is called for.

Pru is determined to see and speak for people that live on the margins of society. She does this by producing work with strong statements and retelling unjust stories that have been forgotten. The poignancy of her work is its greatest strength. Where others would be afraid to tread, Pru does so with determination of voice and a hope that the work sparks even one conversation that may help lessen injustice even a little bit.

Above: Pru with her sketchbook
Opposite, top: Painting on a cast form.

FORM

Stephen Bird

CLAY BODIES: white earthenware; terracotta
SURFACE FINISHES: mixes own maiolica glaze and a low-solubility lead borosilicate clear glaze; a range of metal oxides and stains on glaze enamels
KILN TYPE: electric
FIRING TEMPERATURE/CONE: cone 10

Stephen Bird was born in Stoke-on-Trent, England's centre of pottery. His father worked in the coal mines that provided the fuel for the kilns and, as a child, Stephen played on piles of discarded moulds at a factory that backed onto his grandmother's cottage. You could say he was familiar with ceramics from birth.

In the 1980s, Stephen went to art college in Dundee, Scotland, and majored in painting. For the next decade, he worked almost solely with oil painting. A study trip to the Cyprus College of Art gave him a taste of ceramics, which he explored further when he returned to Scotland. He studied ceramics at Angus College, which was a life-changing experience. Stephen has since given equal time to ceramics and painting. He says the core conversation in his work has been between painting and ceramics and where the two mix.

When he began combining the artforms, he felt as if he was doing something forbidden, invading new territory. Stephen had something to say and knew he could make a bigger impact by combining the mediums. Ceramics was more approachable – it was not only for those interested in 'art'. There was a period in the 1990s when it was financially untenable to buy fine art materials, so he raided bins and used household items to create sculptures and paint over them, including all sorts of found objects in his work.

Stephen visited Australia in 1999 and relocated to Sydney in 2007, establishing a painting and ceramics studio. He is represented in and collected by institutions internationally. He now lives in Mullumbimby, New South Wales, and works in his studio most days. He says his approach to studio time is 'haphazard', but then he quotes a David Whyte poem: 'Start with the first thing close in, the step you don't want to take'. He often reminds himself of this poem because with ceramics all you want to do is get to the fun part, but what is really important, 'is to take the first mundane step, you have to build the base for the sculpture to sit upon'.

He draws a lot so he can get his ideas out of his head. Although there are some he holds on to, allowing them to seep out at the right time.

Stephen handbuilds all his work. For plates, he uses clay slabs pressed into moulds, and for his sculptural work, he forms by hand. He makes many small pieces of sculpture of different objects, which he then combines to make a larger sculpture. Because his larger sculptural pieces are complex, he prefers to think of each small piece by itself first.

His plates have little messages or thoughts that he thinks deserve to be written down. He imagines they have appeared on scraps of paper or pocket notebooks that someone has scribbled on while having the thought. Putting them on a ceramic artwork gives these thoughts a more elevated meaning, because they become permanent through the firing process. At exhibitions, he likes to use the plates to punctuate the space, making people slow down to consider the words and what they mean. They are irreverent, humorous, sad, political, or all of those together, especially when viewed with the illustrations. His intention is to have a conversation through the work.

Stephen makes his own clay moulds by using a lump of clay and carving into it his own patterns and motifs. When bisque fired, he uses them to press into clay to recreate the patterns on any of his work. He loves mixing things up. He uses a combination of drawing, sgraffito and painting styles and has his own recipe for a maiolica glaze, as well as various clay slips with mixes of metal oxides and stains. He layers his illustrative work with attached three-dimensional objects, most of which are unexpected and yet completely deliberate.

Previous: *Pair of boxers,* 2021, glazed earthenware with enamel, 83 x 27 x 22 cm.

Above: *Big head,* 2020, glazed earthenware with lustre, 51 x 43 cm.

Ultimately, Stephen enjoys all the steps of engagement with the clay. At any point, an idea can spring into his mind and he'll follow it. He strives to make something that he never could have imagined. He doesn't like to be defined by one type of clay or process. Born in one of the most traditional pottery towns in the world, Stephen's work is anything but traditional – not in his process, not in his voice, and certainly not in his finished work. It is unique in the best possible way, expertly made and finished, but with that something extra that leaves you thinking.

This page, top to bottom: A collection of toby jugs; a finished piece by Stephen; painting on a sculpted head.

FIRE —— FORM

FIRE — FORM

Clairy Laurence

CLAY BODIES: fine white stoneware
SURFACE FINISHES: underglaze colours; clear glaze; glaze mixed with copper and cobalt carbonate
KILN TYPE: electric
FIRING TEMPERATURE/CONE: cone 8

Clairy Laurence is fascinated by the fact that you can dig up mud and create something with it; put it through the fire and create an object that lasts forever. This sense of wonder about the medium of clay has been with Clairy her whole life.

Clairy grew up in an artistic household – her mother was an artist and a teacher – and this formed who she is. She was not just taught, but shown what was possible. Her long career is proof that she knew what she wanted to achieve and had the dedication to make it happen.

She has made tableware and vessels, but in her current practice she is known for her complex, other-worldly sculptures that draw the viewer in with equal parts mystery and whimsy. As a child, Clairy was drawn to sculptures in galleries rather than paintings, admiring the three-dimensional aspect. It is no coincidence that her practice is sculpture-based. Her creatures – be they fish, monkeys, crocodiles, birds, sacred hearts, skulls or women – all have a face and eyes.

Clairy works from her light-filled home studio in Indooroopilly, Brisbane. It is also a workshop space for the sculpture classes she runs with her niece Libby. She likes the social nature of teaching and sharing her passion with students. Teaching allows her to pass on her love for clay and also keeps her studio sustainable. Her studio is full of tools and moulds she has made herself. She has bowls of clay moulds she has made for many varied eyes, insects, moths and stars. Other bowls are filled with fondant cutters for the many and varied flowers that are a motif in much of her work. There is a wheel and a slab roller, many tables, shelves of brushes and other tools she has collected, adapted or created herself.

The clay she uses isn't suited to coil work so she often works with rolled slabs to create a form. She lets it dry in the sun or uses a heat gun and then, at leather-hard stage, carves it and adds to it with the adornments. Clairy's attention to detail is admirable. She ensures surfaces are smoothed by sponging before she adds underglazes and glazes, or adds the layers of clay motifs she has made, adhering them by scratching both clay pieces and gluing them with slip. She appreciates the different textures that are created in all stages of the making process, carving into leather-hard clay, making marks on floral emblems and attaching beads and glass after the sculptures emerge from the kiln.

Clairy is known for her highly decorated 'babes'. Ornate and often clothed in clay-made florals, these small female sculptures each have their own personality. She uses many complex clay-working techniques to achieve her community of surreal human forms.

She mostly works towards exhibition collections. She often begins working with a drawing, but usually the ideas and concepts she houses in her head lead to an eventual outcome. She gets her hands in the clay and lets the stream of consciousness take over. Her interest in the surrealist movement and a quirky desire to 'put something where it doesn't belong' reflects this curiosity. The natural world features heavily in her designs. Overarching themes include the cycle of life and death and alternative realities, reflecting her interest in philosophy.

Clairy is most excited when she creates new work, and is inspired when her ideas are working and she can see it happening. At this stage, she just wants to keep working, refining the piece and flowing with a theme. However, if a piece of work becomes too pretty or sweet, she pulls the balance back to darker motifs – 'weirds it up a bit' by putting in teeth or adding human ears to a monkey. When she has finished a piece, she detaches herself from it. The piece becomes the story of the viewer or custodian of the piece.

Above, top: Clairy's kiln shed.
Opposite: Sculptures at various drying stages.

Her wondrous creations, be they wistful, sad or cheeky, remind us of something we might not have known or even imagined. This is her strength. With a slight tinge of melancholy, she says there is always part of herself in each sculpture. How lucky we are to know her through her clay imaginings.

Dai Li

CLAY BODIES: fine white stoneware; white raku

SURFACE FINISHES: homemade clear stoneware glaze; iron oxide; high-temperature colour pigments

KILN TYPE: gas

FIRING TEMPERATURE/CONE: cone 10

Looking into the eyes of one of **Dai Li**'s ceramic sculptures, the viewer is struck by the emotion they can see. At once funny, sometimes sad, reflective or cheeky, there is something in her work that draws you in. This is her magic.

Dai Li works from her home studio overlooking the Glasshouse Mountains in the hinterland of Queensland. She starts her day in the studio after her sons go off to school and her partner and fellow artist, Joseph Dawes, heads to his painting studio in another corner of the property. Joseph and Dai Li did once share a studio but their differing musical tastes and need for solitude in the making process was the catalyst for her moving into a closed-in verandah of the house. She makes the most of the time the children are at school and also sometimes works later in the evening, when the house is quiet.

Throughout her schooling in China, and encouraged by her parents, Dai Li learned drawing. This set her up to understand human gestures and form. Later, she discovered clay was her medium of choice. She found working with clay to be soothing, and her happy place. 'When I was very young, every household in my hometown in Sichuan had a pickle jar, which was made of terracotta with a natural ash glaze. The shape was similar to the moon jar. I always loved the look of them.' Dai Li moved to Australia in 2009 and set up her practice, which still includes drawing. She says drawing allows her show more 'space' than a sculpture can.

Her beautiful and sometimes enigmatic female sculptures are handbuilt from a sandy or smooth white stoneware clay and she works on as many as nine at a time over a month. She starts with a rough body shape, then adds the head, often adding the hands at the same time. The gestures, whether touching the face or crossed arms, are part of the story and need to be formed at the same time. She fills the sculptures with newspaper to give the form strength while she moves onto carving the details. The newspaper burns out during the firing.

Dai Li works with wooden tools she brought from China. She also carves her own bamboo tools from branches found on her property. These tools are her mainstay for carving the moods in the faces, and the clothes and accessories of each sculpture.

Her work, including functional wares of cups, jugs and vases, are fired in a gas kiln in her studio and Joseph makes her glazes. She decants and mixes pigments into some of the glazes but also paints with pigments over clear glazes when she wants clearer and more vibrant colours or patterns and decorations to cover the work.

The sad, quirky, dry and sometimes hilarious characters of the women Dai Li portrays in her work come from keen observations. She says they are 'just snippets' of characters she's found solace in and observed in books, films and real life. The characters aren't just born of emotions, they can simply portray physical aspects, such as the way the wind blows on someone's hair, the sunglasses or mask they wear, the raincoat that covers them, a drooping cigarette that hangs from their mouth. The physical plays into the emotional attitude.

Dai Li makes beautiful and thought-provoking women who sit in crystallised glass-glazed bath tubs, hold hands on their hearts or wistfully look somewhere far away. She explains that the Chinese concept of beauty is that it needs to have something melancholic about it to make it more beautiful. Somehow this portrayal of melancholy in her work sits perfectly with the mischievous and light-hearted expressions in her other pieces.

There is no one reason that people find her work so appealing, but she often receives letters from collectors saying that her work has helped them reflect on themselves. Some even say that her work brings them joy. This exchange between maker and observer, be it cheeky or melancholy, is Dai Li's ceramic magic.

Opposite, top left to right: Dai Li's favourite tools; handbuilding body parts for her sculptures.

Dan Elborne

CLAY BODIES: any and all types depending on the project – balance of aesthetics, conceptual or historical unpinning of a chosen topic

SURFACE FINISHES: mixes own conceptually relevant materials to suit the project – colour, tone, luminosity, minerals, metals

KILN TYPE: electric

FIRING TEMPERATURE/CONE: whatever suits each project

For **Dan Elborne**, a project starts with a thought, a conversation or an injustice and keeps developing in his rarely peaceful mind. The use of clay in Dan's work is a given, but what he accomplishes with it is remarkably different to most ceramic work.

Dan came late to the game. He didn't study art at school – he was a confused teenager who loved punk music and illustrated his friends' bands artwork. It was these friends who motivated him to study art. He started with a degree in creative arts at the University of Southern Queensland, followed by an honours year and then a PhD. It is safe to say that Dan found his purpose.

His PhD work, titled *Deathgate*, is a ceramic installation of 1.3 million ceramic 'stones', one for each person detained in the Auschwitz network of concentration camps. Over the course of three years, four months and twenty-four days, he pinched off pieces of various clays and fired them in the large kilns at the university.

The sheer volume of work he was attempting worried his PhD supervisor, who doubted he could achieve it in time. For the duration of the work, Dan did little else other than work a full-time job and make *Deathgate* in the evenings and nights. In the first year, he suffered severe repetitive strain injury to his wrist.

For most artists, a project on this scale would be too much; for Dan, it was a mission to reference the horror of the death camps in a tangible way. Every time he found himself getting distracted, he reminded himself what each stone represented. Every time he packed the kiln, he knew the number of stones represented the number of people who were gassed in Auschwitz.

Each stone bears his fingerprint: a human mark. The size and random shapes of the stones are also representative of the actual stones that surround the train tracks that brought the prisoners into the camps. This series of 1.3 million pieces is a major work that is a much-needed reminder of the horror of our recent history. Its scope means it is not just a representation but a statistical truth. And, of course, ultimately it only references a fraction of the total number of people murdered in the Holocaust. The series was shown at The Goods Shed in Toowoomba, Queensland, and is now in storage waiting to be shown again.

In 2020, just prior to the Covid-19 pandemic, Dan moved to Melbourne and started a series called *Conduit*. His aim is to raise money for victims of domestic violence. It is an issue that was highlighted during his first time living in a big city, with its apartments stacked on top of each other, at a time of collective stress, seeing, hearing and ruminating on what the pressure does to people.

For *Conduit*, Dan is using a slip-cast process to create the forms. He says the objects are almost reductive, simplistic forms. He has reclaimed materials from demolished houses, such as bricks and metal, which he sieves and mixes with a stoneware slip. These materials directly reference the damage done by domestic and family violence. In a clever combination of collectability and commerce used for the greater good, he donates 90 per cent of the total revenue to charity.

Like many artists who connect with clay, Dan says he knew instantly it would be the medium of choice for his work. Clay has a strong connection to history and has been fundamental to our survival. It has been used to create shelter, to transport water and to commemorate and memorialise civilisations, and can be very utilitarian or highly decorative.

Previous, above and opposite:
Stages of Dan's ceramic installation titled *Deathgate*. The installation is comprised of pinched clay stones from wedges of clay, each bearing his fingerprint.

Dan has committed to long-term goals and projects that are altruistic, creating collectable ceramic objects that can raise funds to reduce suffering. This type of long-term work requires great commitment to studio time. He practices most days, although he says he works in short, sharp but consistent bursts, which are decently productive. When asked about the emotional toll of his practice, he says he intentionally contemplates and engages with darkness because it ultimately accentuates the light.

248 DAN ELBORNE

Opposite, top to bottom: Pouring slip into moulds; *Where They Burn Books*, 2020–ongoing, porcelain, paper ash, glaze and gold lustre.

Above: A series of work titled *Conduit* begun in 2020 and made using slip-cast stained stoneware, crushed reclaim from demolished homes, glaze, lustres and custom decals.

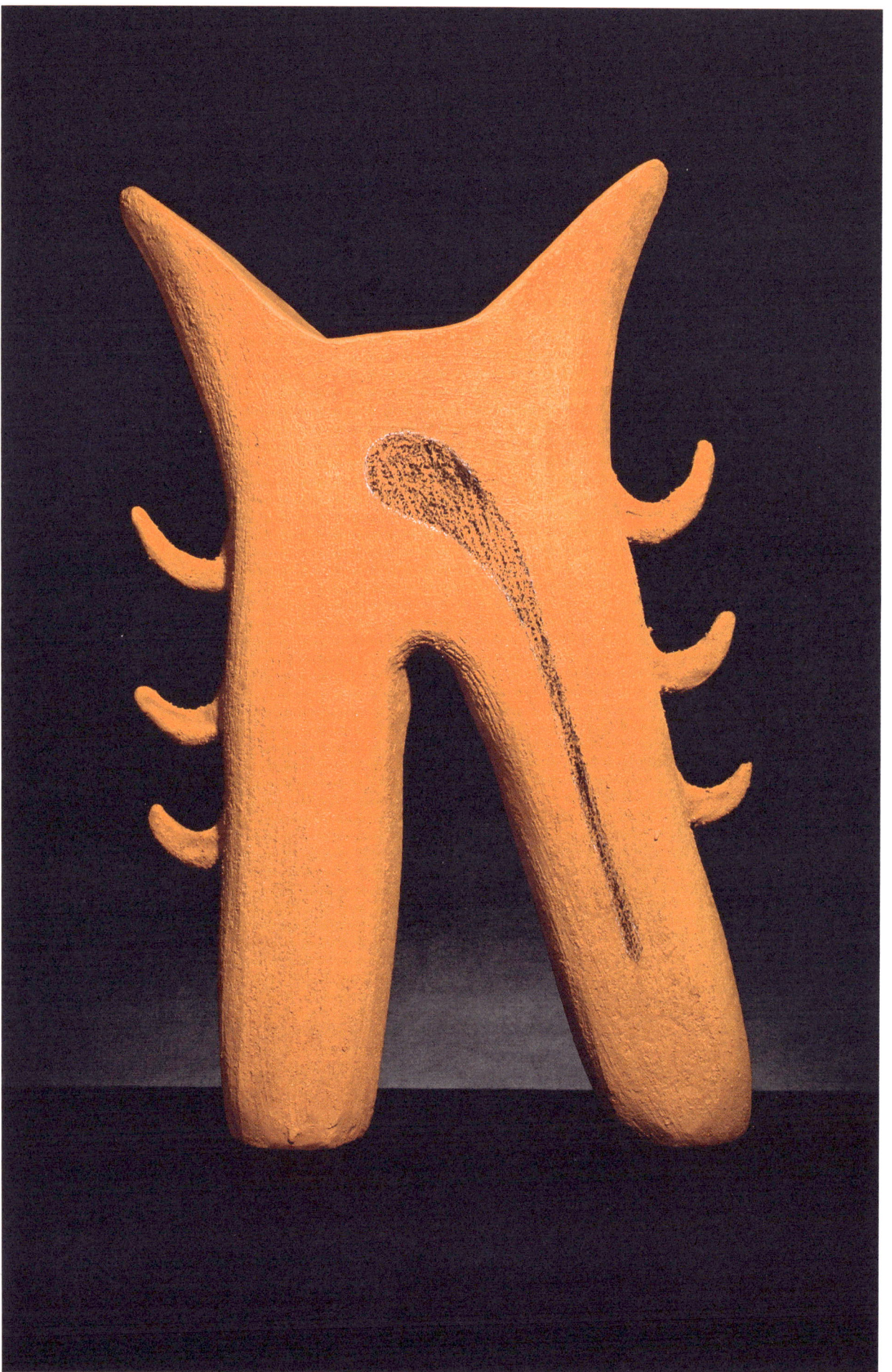

Janet Fieldhouse

CLAY BODIES: mid-fire warm and chocolate brown stoneware; buff raku trachyte; porcelain; Keraflex porcelain

SURFACE FINISHES: stains for colouring porcelain; mixed media

KILN TYPE: electric

FIRING TEMPERATURE/CONE: stoneware 900–1250°C/1652–2282°F, cone 6; porcelain 1280°C/2336°F, cone 9

It seems unrealistic that a potter can work without a studio full of materials and machinery, but **Janet Fieldhouse** has always been able to work, no matter where she is. 'My studio is me.' She bought her first kiln during the Covid-19 pandemic and set up a studio at her home in Cairns, Queensland.

A Torres Strait Islander woman, Janet grew up in Yorkeys Knob, just north of Cairns. As a child, she was inspired to draw by the sailing ships that passed the coast and images of Van Gogh's sunflowers. However, it wasn't until she was in high school that she considered art as a career. She did an associate diploma of cultural arts where she focused on ceramics, learning the mainstream way of making with clay, before beginning to use her own stories in her pieces. Janet become a tutor in that same course, teaching for nine years and encouraging many young Indigenous students to enrol.

When Janet was in her thirties, she took up a six-month scholarship to study ceramics at the Australian National University (ANU) in Canberra. Despite the extreme change in weather, she relished her time at the university, working in the well-resourced studio and meeting students from around the world. She stayed on in Canberra and worked as a cultural arts teacher at Canberra Institute of Technology. She also continued to study at ANU and completed a Master of Philosophy (Visual Arts) degree, writing a thesis that concentrated on Torres Strait Islander women's artefacts. She did research in the Australian Institute of Aboriginal and Torres Strait Islander Studies's Haddon Collection, looking at materials collected in the Torres Strait Islands from 1888 to 1905, where she found a wealth of reference material about her ancestors. She then returned to Cairns, took up a teaching job at her old TAFE and focused on turning her research into art.

Janet uses commercial clays and mixes them with found objects. Her local clay is used in traditional healing and ceremonial rituals, so she chooses not to use it in her work. She mostly handbuilds, although she does use moulds and slip casting when a piece requires it. When she first learned to wheel throw, her instinct was to throw left-handed, something she still does. None of her work is bisque fired and she doesn't glaze her work, preferring to do a single firing and allow the natural texture of the earth to come through.

In one of her earlier works she used Keraflex, a flexible porcelain, to weave ceramic versions of traditional baskets. She first fired it to 1280°C/2336°F and it came out well. However, on the second piece, it over-fired and magic happened in the kiln. The porcelain slumped and showed her what could happen when the temperature was pushed higher. The deformity made for an even more interesting piece, and Janet embraced that mistake as a new process.

She loves that she can manipulate clay and take it to extremes, and that, if it breaks, she can use that experience to make the next version better. But she also loves what she can express using clay. Her work is not just a reflection on her ancestry, it also describes who she is and how she sees herself today – the daughter of a Torres Strait Islander mother and an English-born father who grew up in the Torres Strait and 'knew more than Mum about the place'. Exploring her own multicultural and multigenerational history, Janet uses found objects to tell a more complete story. Emu feathers, shells, tree branches and raffia combine to create a visual history of material cultural items.

Janet's work strikes you in the most profound way: form reflecting function, history and the present, women's sacrifice and her own identity, and the daily life of the Torres Strait. She is interested to learn what people who

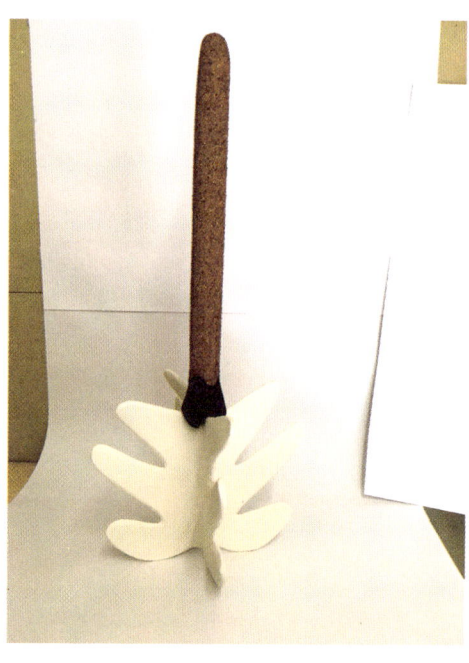

Previous: *Mark and Memory 3*, 2014, red raku, black and white charcoal, 50 x 32 x 11 cm.

Above, top to bottom: Part of the artwork *Hybrid Coconut Scaper Canoe Series 1*, 2019; Janet assembling her artwork titled *Confluence Scarification Hybrids Series 6*.

interact with her work see through their own lens. No matter how personal the piece is to her, she knows people will find their own story within it.

Janet is a storyteller and a historian, as well as a person searching for her own identity. She does this through her art, her mentoring and her teaching. She is an open book and a sponge for knowledge. All of this comes through in her ceramic work. Clay is her canvas, and she uses it beautifully to paint her pictures.

This page, top to bottom: *Bride pendant*, 2014, raku, shell, string, cassowary feathers and beads, 55 x 32 cm; *Scarification Hybrids Series 1*, 2017, chocolate brown, red mid-fire terra, cool ice, 41 x 35 x 14 cm.

Kenji Uranishi

CLAY BODIES: porcelain
SURFACE FINISHES: clear glaze
KILN TYPE: electric
FIRING TEMPERATURE/CONE: 1280°C/2336°F

Kenji Uranishi's work is both precise and fluid. Porcelain lines and curves create unique sculptures. He is inspired by sound and smell, by emotional experiences and memories, and his reflections on these inspirations inform his work. He believes that shapes have emotions attached to them and wants his work to bring an emotional experience to the viewer.

Kenji's work is half handbuilt structures and half made with casts. Each process is done in batches in order to see the finished products through to firing in one workflow. One of the assumptions about his work process is that his planning must be extremely structured. In fact, the opposite is true. He has sketchbooks full of ideas and his most favoured are drawn directly onto his table so he can see the form he is aiming to create. His process is quite unplanned from there.

When starting a handbuilding project, Kenji spends two days at the beginning of the week measuring, rolling and preparing the slabs of clay, keeping them damp under a towel until they are ready. He then begins cutting. Once the trim size of each piece has been decided, he uses a ruler and sharp blade to ensure each small piece is accurate. These pieces sit in his 'damp room' (a plastic box that sits within reach) until he is ready to build a sculpture. When he begins to build, he can finish a sculpture in a day. As he builds the structure, he is in a state of constant curiosity about how it will end up. When it is finished, it is wrapped in plastic and put aside for at least two months to dry well.

Kenji pushes the limits of the clay, often past where he thinks it will work, but he still dares to try. He thinks the limitations of the material are pliable – there is no way to truly know if his structure will be successful until it has been fired. In Kenji's work, it is his risk-taking and boundary-pushing that is most admired.

His other favourite process is slip casting, which he discovered during a residency in Arita, Japan, in 2014. He wanted to learn how to create multiples of his artwork. After spending time with the master mouldmaker, he tried the process himself and immediately knew he had to make it a part of his practice. This new process of carving into the plaster, creating a mould, and duplicating his carvings set him on a path of larger sculptures with more three-dimensional curves and designs.

By creating plaster blocks that he then carves down with a sharp blade, he embraces the element of play, enjoying the feel of the plaster as it carves, the sleek and smooth shapes that he could create with almost total freedom, and the experimentation required to fix anything that goes wrong. The only restraint is to nominate the points where the forms will connect to create the final sculpture, otherwise, Kenji says, he works with 'intuition and hope – not knowing is more interesting.'

The cast method takes much longer than handbuilding, but once the mould is ready, he makes as many sections as the finished sculpture requires. Even if weather permits, he can only produce two sections a day. Timing is crucial when it comes to removing the pieces from the mould, and they sit in his damp box until they are ready to be combined into the final sculpture.

Once all the pieces are finished, he paints the slip onto the required spots to adhere them. He then bisque fires the completed sculpture. After bisque firing, he sand polishes with a diamond file, dips into his glaze, removing glaze with a palette knife from the points he wants to leave raw, and then does a final fire.

In both processes, Kenji achieves a transparency from the pure porcelain clay he cuts his slabs from and from the porcelain slip he makes for the casts. It took trial and error with his electric kiln to get consistency in the glaze across both styles of work, but the effort was worth it to achieve the light blue glaze that is unique to his work.

Previous: Carving plaster to make a mould.

Surprisingly for someone whose work is so pristine, Kenji likes nothing more than getting dirty. When he was at art college in Japan, he was proud to wear his clay-dirtied apron to the cafe, proud that people would know he was a potter.

Kenji's work is widely loved, shown and collected. He has created public art, continues to teach and is still completely in awe of the material. He loves the endless possibilities of the material and embraces the challenges of the technical side. He believes that 'making art is not controlling the material 100 per cent – the random incidents and unexpected outcomes are what makes it more enjoyable'.

This page, clockwise from top: Clay slabs ready to cut and use; individual pieces ready for sculpting; marking and cutting the slab pieces for accuracy.

Nicolette Johnson

CLAY BODIES: ironstone
SURFACE FINISHES: jewel-toned glazes – mottled, speckled, micro-crystalline
KILN TYPE: electric (anagama when possible)
FIRING TEMPERATURE/CONE: cone 10

Nicolette Johnson was born in London, raised in Texas and has lived in Brisbane since 2005. She studied photography at Queensland College of Art but when she embarked on a photography career, she realised it wasn't fulfilling her. In 2015 she started at Clayschool in Brisbane and discovered many things about clay that she loved – opening a bag of clay and smelling the wet earth; how it feels when she is centring a ball on the wheel; how to make marks on clay and seeing evidence of that at the end. It gripped her from the first day of class.

Nicolette was always a collector of things. As a kid it was found things like shells and rocks. When she was older, she was drawn to op shops and vintage stores, shops that sell pieces that someone has loved. 'When something has lasted for a long time and is still in good condition, it means someone has taken care of it and it holds a more emotional connection.' Her collection of found vases is substantial and has been a major influence on her. She sees vases as sculpture. 'They are a holder of space; they both contain a space and take up space at the same time.'

When approaching a new work, she initially sketches it out, then decides on the shape first – long and thin, which she considers more serious, or a larger, more generous and round shape, which she prefers. While she builds the piece, she constantly refers to her sketch but she works by eye and feel, not measurements, adjusting where she feels the piece wants to go.

Nicolette creates her vessels with a combination of wheel throwing and coil building. Starting with the base, she throws to around 10 centimetres high, coils a section and smooths it out with water and slip on the wheel. She has found that throwing in a downwards direction, then up, and repeating that process, bonds the clay and gives the piece a stronger structure. Even though she says she physically couldn't throw a piece that is 60 centimetres tall, by building this way, she is only restricted by the size of her kiln.

She unapologetically says she loves beauty for beauty's sake and does not feel compelled make big statements or share her opinions through her work. She just likes making work that is beautiful. Her forms are certainly that – reimagined ancient forms that have adornments added to give the vessels a contemporary and sculptural finish. Her additions are inspired by a large range of references – the natural world, textiles and patterns, fashion accessories and shapes in jewellery all inform her designs. Along with her choice of glaze colours and oxides, Nicolette achieves a look that is entirely her own.

Once made, the vessel is covered in plastic and allowed to dry slowly, often for a few weeks, then bisque fired in an electric kiln. At the glazing stage, she prefers to full dip the pots, but if the glaze is too runny, she paints it on the top and sponges it around the bottom to get the consistency of coverage right. Depending on the pot, she will fire two or three times, adding a layer of glaze each time. The layers of glaze and the magic of the heat give the vessel a sense of depth.

The result is not always successful or what she expected, but she allows herself to fix problems along the way and accept the end result as part of the process. She concedes she wants everything to be perfect, but she has to draw a line. She loves knowing that a shape she made by a certain movement of her body while wheel throwing and what she adds with her hands will be proof of her existence forever. Clay allows her to truly enjoy work as pure fun with no baggage, just total creative release.

Previous and opposite: Using various tools to add adornments to the vessels.

FIRE —— FORM

Opposite: Pieces drying in Nicolette's home studio.

Sassy Park

CLAY BODIES: terracotta; white raku; mid- and high-fire porcelain
SURFACE FINISHES: watercolour underglazes (mixed and bought); oxides; stains; maiolica; clear glazes
KILN TYPE: electric, woodfire and reduction (when possible)
FIRING TEMPERATURE/CONE: 900–1280°C/1652–2336°F

Sassy Park is an artist who uses ceramics as a medium, rather than a ceramic artist. Her ceramic work is varied in form: sculptures delicately painted with watercolour underglazes, terracotta amphoras with words painted around the body, and thrown plates with sad truths and pretty illustrations forming a dichotomy between the melancholy of the words and the beauty of the imagery.

Sassy studied art at the Sydney College of the Arts and majored in painting. After being a painter for twenty years, and having a family, she found her stride in ceramics when she did a master's degree in ceramics at the National Art School in Sydney. Now, ideas that were once formed in her paintings are coming back into her ceramic work.

Working most days, Sassy splits her time between her home studio, where she paints and writes, and a shared studio space, kil.n.it, in Glebe, an inner-city district of Sydney, where she does most of her making – mainly handbuilding, but also throwing, slip casting and mould making.

Her work usually has a quiet meaning: the title of a piece explaining what is expressed in the forms, or the literal meaning of words she inscribes. Her text-based works often carry phrases she finds interesting in a film or a book or in daily life. These texts bring to life a small moment that might otherwise go unnoticed, giving them a place to live in a different form. She is interested in things that are forgotten and the small things that go on around us every day: daily life, the news, stereotypes, taboos.

Sassy also reacts to situations that she finds cathartic, funny, melancholy or perplexing, and finds a way to express them in words. Some examples are 'Ceramics suit me because I'm used to disappointment', 'Woman of sorrows' and 'She lost her composure 6 January 2020'. They also range from irreverent – 'I don't want Jesus to love me' (a reaction to a large sign at a church she passes daily) – to political – 'Stop shagging men' (a comment on the unfortunate things that happen to women in politics).

She insists the texts are not meant to be didactic or judgemental, but questioning. For her, putting text on a plate, which is a very domestic object, is a form of humanity. The humble plate says something and is understood.

Sassy views her sculpted figures depicting the rich history of people and animals as another form of humanity. If we understand the vessel, we understand the figure – they are domestic and human and we see 'what they are'. The vessels and sculptures she makes and writes on are statements in themselves.

She uses myriad techniques and likes the problem-solving that clay as a medium demands. She plans her work by drawing it out first, honing her ideas as her imagery and thoughts come from many places and sources. She uses a large range of clay bodies, including terracotta, white raku and porcelains, and she both mid-fires and high-fires. She uses a variety of finishes, from majolica to unglazed, watercolour-like oxides to stains.

Always thinking about how to achieve her vision for her work and make it look a certain way, she sees every piece as a challenge. If it were easy, she wouldn't do it.

For Sassy, ceramics are ultimately a fragile medium and human existence is also fragile. It's theories like this she embodies in her work and hopes to share with the custodians of her pieces.

Above, bottom: Sassy painting on a vessel.
Opposite: Collected works and a sculptured bust drying in her home studio.

Index of artists

STEPHEN BIRD 231
Website: stephenbird.net
Instagram: stephen_bird_artist
Work available through Olsen Gallery (New South Wales), Scott Livesey Galleries (Victoria), The Scottish Gallery (Edinburgh)

BRIDGET BODENHAM 41
Website: bridgetbodenham.com
Instagram: bridgetbodenham
Work available through the artist's online store

SANDRA BOWKETT 157
Website: sandrabowkett.com
Instagram: sandrabowkett
Work available online and through Craft Victoria, Mr Kitly (Victoria), Shepparton Art Museum (Victoria) and The Plant Society (Australia, Japan)

KATE BOWMAN 61
Website: katebowmanceramics.com
Instagram: katebowmanceramics
Work available through Stoker Studio (Victoria), JamFactory (South Australia) and Alba Thermal Springs (Victoria)

KEVIN BOYD 149
Instagram: kevinboydceramics
Work available through Skepsi Gallery (Victoria)

RAY CAVILL 153
Website: raycavill.com
Instagram: cavillray

ZAK CHALMERS 175
Website: valleyplainspottery.com.au
Instagram: valleyplainspottery.com.au
Work available through the artist's online store and the Valley Plains Pottery studio and gallery (Victoria)

CARA EDWARDS 93
Website: caraedwardsdesign.com
Instagram: caraedwardsdesign
Work available through the artist's online store

DAN ELBORNE 245
Website: danelborne.studio
Instagram: danelborne
Work available from the artist

MEL ELIADES 109
Website: claybeehive.com
Instagram: claybeehive
Work available through the artist's online store, collaborations with various other businesses, and wholesale through Seventh Pocket (Victoria), Eva's Sunday (Victoria), Boom Gallery (Victoria) and mondocherry (Victoria)

PENNY EVANS 219
Website: pennyevansart.com
Instagram: pennyevansart

JANET FIELDHOUSE 251
Website: janetfieldhouse.website
Instagram: janetfieldhouse
Work available through Vivien Anderson Gallery (Victoria)

HONOR FREEMAN 129
Website: honorfreeman.com/
Instagram: honor.freeman
Work available through Sabbia Gallery (New South Wales)

SUSAN FROST 167
Website: susanfrostceramics.com
Instagram: susanfrost
Work available through the artist's online store

IRENE GRISHIN-SELZER 193
Website: wirenegrishinselzer.com and iggyandloulou.com
Instagram: irenegrishinselzer and iggyandloulou
Work available through the artist's online stores, Modern Times (Victoria) and pépite (Victoria)

BONNIE HISLOP 87
Website: bonniehislop.com and dabblerstudio.com
Instagram: bonnie_hislop
Work available through the artist's online store

NIHARIKA HUKKU 213
Website: niharikahukku.com
Instagram: niharikahukku

NICOLETTE JOHNSON 261
Website: nicolettejohnsonceramics.com
Instagram: nicolette__johnson
Work available through the artist's online store

CLAIRY LAURENCE 237
Website: clairylaurence.com
Instagram: clairylaurence
Work available through Lamington (Queensland), JamFactory (South Australia) and artisan (Queensland)

AMY LEEWORTHY 183
Website: amyleeworthy.com
Instagram: amyleeworthy
Work available through the artist's online store

DAI LI 241
Website: etsy.com/shop/dailijewellery
Instagram: dai_li_ and dailijewellery
Artwork available through Jan Manton Gallery (Queensland), Beaver Galleries (Canberra), Bett Gallery (Tasmania) and The Gallery Eumundi (Queensland). Ceramic functional wares and jewellery available through paper boat press (Queensland), MoB Shop (Queensland), artisan (Queensland), Scarlet Jones (Victoria) and Beaver Galleries (Canberra).

ERIN LIGHTFOOT 123
Website: erinlightfoot.com
Instagram: erinlightfoot_porcelain
Work available online and through gift and gallery stores around Australia

REBECCA LINDEMANN 71
Website: spunmud.com.au
Instagram: spun_mud
Work available through Eumundi Market (Queensland), GOMA Design Market (Queensland) and Finders Keepers Market (Victoria)

YEN YEN LO 117
Website: yenyenlo.wixsite.com/pinch/home
Instagram: yen.yen.lo
Work available through the artist's online store

SANDY LOCKWOOD 161
Website: sandylockwood.com.au
Instagram: slockwood737
Work available through Schaller Gallery (USA), Stratford Gallery (UK), MIAR Ceramics & Arts (UK) and Sturt Gallery (New South Wales), JamFactory (South Australia), MAKERS GALLERY (Queensland) and Living Clay

ANGUS McDIARMID 143
Website: panpottery.com
Instagram: panpottery
Work available through Belmondos Organic Market (Queensland), Mast Furniture (Queensland), Institute of Modern Art (Queensland), Braer Studio (New South Wales), Newrybar Merchants (New South Wales), Orchard Street Gallery (New South Wales) and Koskela

KATE McKAY 67
Website: katemckayceramics.com.au
Instagram: kate_mckay_ceramics
Work available through the artist's online store

ASUKA MEW 35
Website: wingnutand.co
Instagram: wingnutandco
Work available through the artist's online store and Mr Kitly (Victoria)

PRU MORRISON 225
Website: prumorrison.com
Instagram: prumorrison
Work available through the Institute of Modern Art (Queensland) and artisan (Queensland)

JO NORTON 57
Website: thrownbyjo.com
Instagram: thrownbyjo
Work available through Kira & Kira (Queensland), Our Little Flower Farm (New South Wales) and Tweed Regional Gallery (New South Wales); commissions taken directly

JENNIFER ORLAND 105
Website: jenniferorland.com
Instagram: jenniferorland
Work available through the artist's online store and paper boat press (Queensland)

SERENA PANGESTU AND ANIKA KALOTAY 75
Website: kurastudio.com
Instagram: kura_studio
Work available through the artist's online store and various stockists, including Stackwood (Western Australia), Fremantle Arts Centre (Western Australia), Loam (Western Australia), Namu Leather Goods (Queensland), Miss Arthur (Tasmania), Makers' Mrkt (Victoria) and Black Blaze (New South Wales)

SASSY PARK 267
Website: sassyjpark.com
Instagram: sassypark
Work available through Robin Gibson Gallery (New South Wales) and other exhibitions

LAURA PASCOE 201
Website: brushandwheel.com.au and vacantassembly.com
Instagram: brushandwheel
Work available through Brush & Wheel, various art exhibitions and pop-ups at Vacant Assembly (Queensland) and Open House West End (Queensland)

KIRSTEN PERRY 133
Website: kirstenperry.com
Instagram: kirstenpp
Work available through Mr Kitly (Victoria), Craft Victoria, pépite (Victoria), Boom Gallery (Victoria) and Modern Times (Victoria)

MEL ROBSON 205
Website: melrobson.com
Instagram: melrobsonceramics
Work available through the artist's online store

NAOKO RODGERS 209
Website: etsy.com/shop/dotsandlines10to1000
Instagram: dotsandlines10to1000
Work available from the artist's online store, paper boat press (Queensland), Biku Furniture & Homewares (Queensland), Michael Reid (New South Wales) and Archway (Japan)

JANE SAWYER 51
Website: janesawyer.com.au
Instagram: janesawyer1
Work available through the artist's website, Slow Clay Centre (Victoria) and Craft Victoria

ANNA SCHEEN 83
Website: annascheen.com.au
Instagram: anna_scheen
Work available through the artist's online store, Foy St studio (via appointment Monday–Saturday) and regular events (see website and Instagram for details)

ARCADIA SCOTT 31
Website: arcadiascott.com
Instagram: arcadia_scott
Work available through the artist's online store and various stockists

ROSHNI SENAPATI 113
Website: roshnisenapati.com.au
Instagram: roshni_senapati
Work available through MAKERS GALLERY (Queensland) and direct contact with the artist

HYEYOUN SHIN 101
Website: illyswall.com.au
Instagram: illyswall
Work available through the artist's Etsy store, paper boat press (Queensland), artisan (Queensland), MoB Shop (Queensland), QAGOMA Store (Queensland) and Field Trip Balhannah (South Australia)

ULRICA TRULSSON 171
Website: ulricatrulsson.com
Instagram: ulricatrulsson
Work available through Sabbia Gallery (New South Wales) and Beaver Galleries (Canberra)

CLARE UNGER 97
Website: clareungerceramics.com
Instagram: clare_unger
Work available through Object Shop (Australian Design Centre, Victoria), JamFactory (South Australia) and The Possibility Project (New South Wales)

KENJI URANISHI 255
Website: kenjiuranishi.com.au
Instagram: kamenendo
Work available through the artist's online store

DAVID USHER 189
Website: David-usher.com
Instagram: the_david_usher
Work available through Alexandra Lawson Gallery (Queensland)

HAYLEY A. WEST 47
Website: hayleyawest.com (exhibition work), wellsstreetstudio.com (classes and domestic ware)
Instagram: hayley.a.west
Work available through the artist's online store

KATHERINE WHEELER 197
Website: katherinewheeler.com.au
Instagram: katherinewheeler.com.au
Work available through the artist's online store

INDEX OF ARTISTS

ACKNOWLEDGEMENTS

We are incredibly thankful to the artists who agreed to be part of this book for their openness and candour about their working practices and materials. We enjoyed getting to know each of you and hope that we have done you and your artistry justice. Thank you for supplying photographs and pieces of work for us to photograph. Your generosity of spirit speaks volumes about the ceramics community – we cannot thank you enough. To the team at Thames & Hudson and our publisher, Kirsten Abbott, thank you for asking us to write this book at the right time to celebrate contemporary ceramics in Australia. To Lisa Schuurman, Lorna Hendry, Caitlin O'Reardon and Ashlea O'Neill, thank you for the editorial, production and design genius it takes to bring it all to life. And to Angus Ross and Michael Critchley at Colour Chiefs, thank you for your colour expertise and your ongoing support.

To our family – Bob, Cheryll and Luke – it is your love and support that gets us through. From providing editorial guidance to bringing us soup on winter days when we were stuck at the computer, every single thing made it possible for us to complete this book. Thank you, we love you. Mum and Dad, when you threw your first pot over fifty years ago, would you ever have thought your daughters would write a book on ceramics? Thank you again for instilling in us the love of things both beautiful and useful.

And to our dear friends, extended family and the team at paper boat press – we don't think you realise the extent to which your support is needed or how grateful we are for it. It is, and we really are!

To all the collectors of ceramics – we need you for this industry to not just exist but thrive! Please continue buying handmade functional wares, adorning your homes with beautiful vessels and bringing three-dimensional art into your lives.

Kylie and Tiffany

IMAGE CREDITS

Chapter openers: Kylie Johnson, Tiffany Johnson; **Foreword:** Simon Strong; **Stephen Bird:** Sarah Benton, Olsen Gallery, Stephen Bird; **Bridget Bodenham:** Holly Howe; **Sandra Bowkett:** Sandra Bowkett, Robyn Phelan, Lara Merrington, Elizabeth Masters; **Kate Bowman:** Kate Bowman, Janis House; **Kevin Boyd:** Kevin Boyd, Jack Balfour; **Ray Cavill:** Jen Hillhouse, Ray Cavill; **Zak Chalmers:** Elise Daley, Tanya Chalmers; **Cara Edwards:** Fin Fagan; **Dan Elborne:** Flick Smith, Jemma Cotter, Dan Elborne; **Mel Eliades:** Mel Eliades; **Penny Evans:** Penny Evans, K/Gamilaroi people, work in progress, Widjabal Wia-bal Country/Lismore, New South Wales, 2021, image courtesy National Gallery of Australia, Kamberri/Canberra © the artist; **Janet Fieldhouse:** Fany Saumure, Janet Fieldhouse, Bryna Bamberry; **Honor Freeman:** Alex Beckett, Angus Lee Forbes, Sam Roberts, Grant Hancock; **Susan Frost:** Susan Frost; **Irene Grishin-Selzer:** Irene Grishin-Selzer; **Bonnie Hislop:** Melanie Hinds; **Niharika Hukku:** Niharika Hukku; **Nicolette Johnson:** Nicolette Johnson; **Clairy Laurence:** Kylie Johnson; **Amy Leeworthy:** Amy Leeworthy, Bobby Clark; **Dai Li:** Dai Li, Joseph Daws; **Erin Lightfoot:** Deny Ryan, George Levy, Tang Oudomvilay; **Rebecca Lindemann:** Ketakii Jewson-Brown; **Yen Yen Lo:** Tatanja Ross; **Sandy Lockwood:** Michael Wee, Sandy Lockwood; **Angus McDiarmid:** Bridget McDiarmid; **Kate McKay:** Fliss Dodd, Alan Howard; **Asuka Mew:** Anna Miller-Yeaman; **Pru Morrison:** Kylie Johnson, Tiffany Johnson; **Jo Norton:** Sabine Bannard, Thomas Norton; **Jennifer Orland:** Kylie Johnson, Tiffany Johnson; **Serena Pangestu and Anika Kalotay:** Serena Pangestu, Anika Kalotay; **Sassy Park:** Sassy Park; **Laura Pascoe:** Kylie Johnson, Tiffany Johnson; **Kirsten Perry:** Martina Gemmola; **Mel Robson:** Mel Robson; **Naoko Rodgers:** Kylie Johnson, Tiffany Johnson; **Jane Sawyer:** Peter Bonifacio; **Anna Scheen:** Anna Scheen; **Arcadia Scott:** Martina Gemmola; **Roshni Senapati:** Kylie Johnson; **Hyeyoun Shin:** Kylie Johnson, Tiffany Johnson; **Ulrica Trulsson:** Kylie Johnson, Tiffany Johnson; **Clare Unger:** Flore Vallery-Radot; **Kenji Uranishi:** Kylie Johnson, Tiffany Johnson; **David Usher:** Russell Shakespeare, Kylie Johnson; **Hayley A. West:** Hayley A. West; **Katherine Wheeler:** Holly Howe

First published in Australia in 2023
by Thames & Hudson Australia Pty Ltd
11 Central Boulevard, Portside Business Park
Port Melbourne, Victoria 3207
ABN: 72 004 751 964

First published in the United Kingdom in 2023
by Thames & Hudson Ltd
181a High Holborn
London WC1V 7QX

First published in the United States of America in 2023
by Thames & Hudson Inc.
500 Fifth Avenue
New York, New York 10110

Earth & Fire © Thames & Hudson Australia 2023
Text © Kylie Johnson and Tiffany Johnson 2023
Foreword © Vipoo Srivilasa 2023
Earth & fire: A partnership © Jane Sawyer 2023
The language of clay © Stephanie Outridge Field 2023

Copyright in all texts, artworks and images is held by the creators or their representatives, unless otherwise stated.

26 25 24 23   5 4 3 2 1

The moral right of the authors has been asserted. All rights reserved. No part of this publication may be reproduced or transmitted in any form or by any means, electronic or mechanical, including photocopy, recording or any other information storage or retrieval system, without prior permission in writing from the publisher.

Any copy of this book issued by the publisher is sold subject to the condition that it shall not by way of trade or otherwise be lent, resold, hired out or otherwise circulated without the publisher's prior consent in any form or binding or cover other than that in which it is published and without a similar condition including these words being imposed on a subsequent purchaser.

Thames & Hudson Australia wishes to acknowledge that Aboriginal and Torres Strait Islander people are the first storytellers of this nation and the traditional custodians of the land on which we live and work. We acknowledge their continuing culture and pay respect to Elders past, present and future.

ISBN 978-1-760-76352-7
ISBN 978-1-760-76374-9 (U.S. edition)

 A catalogue record for this book is available from the National Library of Australia

British Library Cataloguing-in-Publication Data
A catalogue record for this book is available from the British Library

Library of Congress Control Number 2022951972

Every effort has been made to trace accurate ownership of copyrighted text and visual materials used in this book. Errors or omissions will be corrected in subsequent editions, provided notification is sent to the publisher.

Design: Ashlea O'Neill | Salt Camp Studio
Editing: Lorna Hendry
Printed and bound in China by 1010 Printing International Limited.

FSC® is dedicated to the promotion of responsible forest management worldwide. This book is made of material from FSC®-certified forests and other controlled sources.

Be the first to know about our new releases, exclusive content and author events by visiting
thamesandhudson.com.au
thamesandhudson.com
thamesandhudsonusa.com